THE
LIVING WILL
HANDBOOK

THE
LIVING WILL
HANDBOOK

The Right to Decide Your Own Fate

ALAN D. LIEBERSON
M.D., J.D., FACP

HASTINGS HOUSE *Book Publishers*
141 Halstead Avenue, Mamaroneck, NY 10543

Library of Congress Catalog Card Number 91-73925

ISBN 0-8038-9334-5

Published in the United States by
Hastings House Book Publishers
141 Halstead Avenue
Mamaroneck, NY 10543

Distributed by Publishers Group West, Emeryville, California

Text design by Irving Perkins Associates
Cover design by Cindy LaBreacht

3   5   7   9   10   8   6   4   2

IN APPRECIATION

I wish to thank my father, Dr. Abraham Lieberson, for encouraging me to question even the obvious; my uncle, David Liberson, for encouraging me to put my thoughts on paper; my wife, Rhona Derrin Lieberson, for accepting my dedication to time to write; and my publisher, Hy Steirman, for extending his editorial skill to eliminate at least some of my circuitous style.

CONTENTS

In developing *The Living Will Handbook*, we have relied heavily on interpreting the common law of the various states and predicting how other state courts are likely to rule given various clinical situations in the future. Obviously, as these interpretations are our own, we cannot guarantee that our suggestions would be accepted by the courts of any particular state now or in the future.

We have also attempted to structure the comprehensive Living Will form to avoid potential problems by including a severability clause, but even this may not be accepted.

Because of this uncertainty of the common law and the variations between jurisdictions, we advise you to review the completed document with an attorney licensed to practice in the state in which you are likely to receive care.

—ALAN D. LIEBERSON

INTRODUCTION

All Americans have the legal right to decide what medical treatment they wish to receive. They usually choose a specific course of treatment after discussing the benefits and risks with their physicians. Often the nature of one's illness affects the patient's ability to make such decisions. However, the legal right to determine one's health care can be maintained even *after* the patient's mental or physical ability to communicate is impaired.

This right is preserved with a Living Will—a document written one day, one week, one, five, ten, or twenty years prior to the onset of the illness. A Living Will provides a series of written instructions to doctors as to what care the patient wishes to accept or reject. The doctor is legally obliged to follow the patient's instructions, even when the patient is no longer able to act for himself or herself.

The Living Will relieves loved ones of the burden of having to make difficult decisions and alleviates the legal and social pressures which foster extended care beyond the point deemed desirable by the patient.

Because numerous "ready-to-use" existing Living Wills are either inadequate or incomplete, the purpose of this book is to inform you and to help you avoid pitfalls in preparing a Living Will. You should spend adequate time to allow for emotional commitment to deal with the important issues which must be addressed when preparing a Living Will.

MEDICAL BACKGROUND

Western society stresses the sanctity of life. As a result American medicine developed an approach to health care which fostered the preservation of life even when the quality of life was limited. Gradually, maintaining life became an end in itself. The death of a patient became a sign of a physician's defeat, the prolonging of life a sign of his or her ability.

This approach served society well until the 1960s when modern technology began to produce machines such as lung and heart machines capable of taking over normal body functions for long periods of time. These machines were intended for temporary use until the normal organ function could be restored and the patient could return to normal life. But the machines also created two major problems.

First, because prolonging life became an end in itself, some physicians employed these machines even in situations in which there was no hope of the patient ever returning to a meaningful life.

Second, even those physicians who avoided unwarranted use of the machines found that emergency circumstances often required the immediate use of such machines when the doctors were unable to determine the potential for a return to meaningful life. When time proved the patient would not get better, the machines, already in use, were difficult to disconnect.

LEGAL BACKGROUND

Along with the development of high-tech medical machines, two legal concepts that would have great impact on Living Wills began to emerge. The first concept was part of the expanding notion of individual rights, which was evolving to include a right of self-determination in health care. The second concept involved the rapid rise in medical malpractice litigation, which scared doctors and hospitals.

The case that brought attention to the need for Living Wills occurred in 1976. Karen Quinlan, a young woman whose brain had been severely injured leaving her in a coma, had been maintained on an artificial respirator for one year. Her parents asked a judge of the New Jersey court to allow them to order her respirator removed.

Amid media headlines and passionate debate across the country, the New Jersey Supreme Court ruled that Karen Quinlan was unable to comprehend her situation or have a voice in the decision. The court allowed her parents, as her closest living relatives, to make the decision for her. Thus began the evolution of the modern legal concept of the right of self-determination in health care.

Meanwhile the concept of malpractice was evolving. Malpractice presumes that there is a medical standard of care by which a physician's actions can be judged. This concept basically says that an individual physician should do what the majority of the physicians do in specific situations. Doctors who followed this standard of care were considered to have acted correctly. Deviation from such standards suggested that the physicians had acted negligently.

But standard care involved prolonging life, even meaningless life, while stopping treatment with the knowledge that doing so would result in death was certainly against the majority approach. Therefore a doctor or hospital who withheld or withdrew medical care that prolonged life easily could be viewed as practicing in a negligent manner.

These two legal concepts were in conflict. The family tells the physician to withhold or withdraw care because the patient will never return to a meaningful life; the doctor feels he can not comply because doing so is against the standard medical practice and would invite a lawsuit.

THE PROBLEM

At present, Living Wills fall under the separate jurisdictions of each state along with Puerto Rico and the District of Columbia (Washington, D.C). Some states have passed laws dealing with "death with dignity" issues, some states have not. In 1990 when the matter of *Cruzan* v *Director, Missouri Department of Health* came before the U.S. Supreme Court, the court chose not to simplify this whole area of law. Instead of addressing the "death with dignity" issues in a decision which would have held priority in all courts and set precedence for untold decisions in the future, it chose to evade the major issue and returned future major decision making to the various state jurisdictions.

Law professors point out that civil rights are traditionally developed slowly through state court decisions and only set into state or federal statutory law after extensive consideration in many courts.

To understand the difficulty and confusion surrounding "death with dignity" issues and the various viewpoints stated in each state's statutes, let's review the final chapter of Karen Quinlan's life.

After the court decision, as per her parents' wishes, Karen's physicians stopped the respirator. Everyone believed she was dependent on the machine to breathe—but they were wrong. In fact, Karen had a medical condition referred to as a persistent vegetative state. In such a condition, the body can survive as long as it is given sustenance—food and water—but the patient is devoid of the ability to think or perceive what is happening in the surroundings. Karen lived another six years in this state, without regaining consciousness or having a relationship to her loved ones or her environment.

Karen's history points out the problem with Living Will statutes and how most of the public and professionals think about Living Wills. The legal right of self-determination in medical care is extensive, but legislators in many states have written Living Will statutes which only cover a small portion of that right. Karen Quinlan did not have a terminal disease, as defined in most Living Will statutes. Furthermore, she was not being kept alive by modern technology. She was being kept alive by the artificial maintenance of nutrition, a procedure which has been used for many decades.

The appropriate intent of the legislative act should be to preserve the patient's right of self-determination in health care. It should be just that, not the much more limited right to stop technology when the person has a terminal disease. To understand this aim we must look at the broader reaches of this right of self-determination in health care.

Section One

THE RIGHT OF SELF-DETERMINATION IN HEALTH CARE

THE CALIFORNIA NATURAL DEATH ACT

In 1976 the California legislature passed the first Living Will Act. It was appropriately called the California Natural Death Act, and it was passed with the intent of allowing the individual the right to die naturally, without unwanted medical interference.

As legislatures frequently do when initiating new legal approaches to society's problems, the California legislature began the Act with an explanation of its objectives and reasons it felt such an act was necessary. This statement, referred to as the "legislative intent," reads as follows:

The legislature finds that adult persons have the fundamental right to control the decisions relating to the tendering of their own medical care, including the decision to have life-sustaining procedures withheld or withdrawn in instances of terminal condition.

The legislature further finds that modern medical technology has made possible the artificial prolongation of human life beyond natural limits.

The legislature finds that, in the interest of protecting individual autonomy, such prolongation of life for persons with terminal condition may cause loss of patient dignity and unnecessary pain and suffering, while providing nothing medically necessary or beneficial to the patient.

The legislature further finds that there exists considerable uncertainty in the medical and legal professions as to the legality of terminating the use or application of life-sustaining procedures where the patient has voluntarily and in sound mind evidenced a desire that such procedures be withheld or withdrawn.

In recognition of the dignity and privacy which patients have a right to expect, the legislature hereby declares that the laws of the State of California shall recognize the right of an adult person to make a written directive instructing the physician to withhold or withdraw life-sustaining procedures in the event of a terminal condition.

THE BROADER PICTURE

The chart on page 14 illustrates the breakdown of the individual's right of self-determination in health care. The whole rectangle represents the broadest possible interpretation. The left side of the rectangle represents health-care decisions that can be made by a competent patient. The right side of the rectangle represents health-care decisions that can be made by an incompetent patient who had written a Living Will when he or she was still competent.

Note there are two large bands and a third smaller band across the top of the rectangle. The large bands represent mercy killing (euthanasia) and suicide, neither of which is legal in America even though they could be considered the expression of a right of self-determination in health care. These acts are accepted in some countries. The third band represents a small number of situations in which the law prohibits even a competent person from making a decision contrary to standard medical care because of counterbalancing state interests (which will be discussed later in

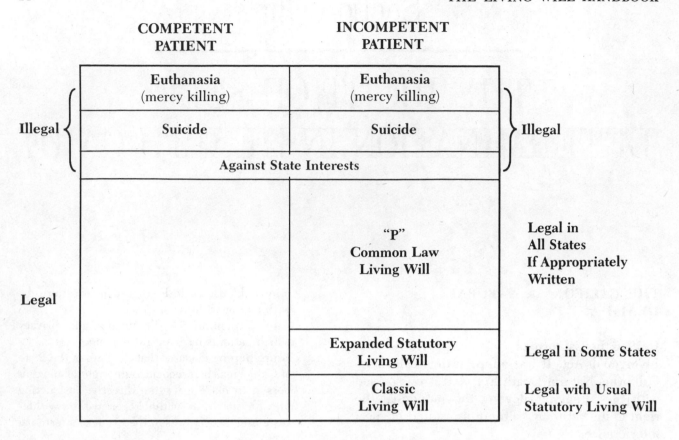

	COMPETENT PATIENT	INCOMPETENT PATIENT	
Illegal {	Euthanasia (mercy killing)	Euthanasia (mercy killing)	} Illegal
	Suicide	Suicide	
	Against State Interests		
Legal		"P" Common Law Living Will	Legal in All States If Appropriately Written
		Expanded Statutory Living Will	Legal in Some States
		Classic Living Will	Legal with Usual Statutory Living Will

the book). These bands apply to both the competent and the incompetent patients.

Next, note that the left side of the rectangle below the bands is totally open. This indicates that competent patients have the right, and the ability, to make any other medical decisions of any type. They can choose whether or not to go for an annual physical. They can choose whether or not to take their insulin. They can accept or refuse open heart surgery, shock therapy, antibiotics, a mammogram, or a CAT scan. As we will see, they can also refuse to have a leg amputated or demand that a respirator be stopped, even though it will result in their own death. The competent person is given his or her full right of self-determination in health care, as indicated by the large open space in the lower two-thirds of the left side of the illustration.

In contrast, note the bands depicted in the lower two-thirds of the right side of the illustration, all of which represent the legal rights of the incompetent patient to make medical decisions.

The bottom band represents the rights contained in a typical Living Will statute, while the next band represents the rights protected under some of the newer Living Will statutes which are written to include patients in the persistent vegetative state and/or to allow the discontinuation of nutrition and hydration. There still remains a large space, marked "P," which represents the problem. It represents all the other rights of the incompetent patient to continue to control his or her destiny not covered by typical Living Wills. These areas need to be addressed.

THE SOLUTION

It is necessary to write a Living Will that addresses whatever areas of medical care you want covered. You have that right. If you demand it and your document is drafted correctly, the law will see that it is honored.

Section Two

BE CAREFUL!
NOT ALL LIVING WILLS ARE
ALIKE

A Living Will may contain any directive you wish as long as it is legal. Most people write Living Wills to direct physicians to discontinue prolonged medical treatment if medical conditions clearly indicate there is no possibility of a return to a meaningful life.

It is unfortunate that most Living Will forms now being distributed cover only a small percentage of the situations in which such undesired care occurs. This situation exists because these Living Will forms cover medical conditions classified as "terminal" as narrowly defined by state laws. As defined by the states, "terminal" conditions usually do not include those clinical situations in which artificial life-support systems are used for prolonged periods, such as:

- Permanent unconsciousness (coma and persistent vegetative state)
- End-stage mental deterioration (Alzheimer's disease, multi stroke, and other dementias)
- Multiple sclerosis, muscular dystrophy, and other progressive, neuro-muscular diseases
- Paraplegia
- End-stage lung, heart, kidney, or liver failure
- AIDS
- Strokes

Because these common conditions are not considered "terminal" under the definition, the intent of the declarant (the signer of the Living Will) to avoid unwanted care is negated. For example, a physician confronted with a now incom-petent patient who had previously executed a Living Will can not honor the patient's directives because the Living Will does not cover the existing condition. When situations such as this arise, the patient loses the right of self-determination, and family and friends are left unprotected and angry. When these cases are made public, the medical profession is criticized in the mistaken belief that the doctors have failed to honor the patient's wishes. The result is the public perception that a Living Will is not worth executing. In fact, a doctor who is fully prepared to honor the patient's directives is bound by the narrowly defined law unless the Living Will covers the specific clinical situations that arise.

When a particular clinical situation exists, a properly worded Living Will should spell out the patient's wishes exactly. Under these circumstances the patient's directives will be routinely honored by physicians and the courts. It is only when the document is poorly worded or has not been drafted to cover specific clinical situations that problems arise.

Illness or accident may strike when one is travelling out of state or even out of the country. Because it is impossible to predict where the declarant may eventually receive medical care, the Living Will document must be signed and witnessed so it is valid in all states plus the District of Columbia, and even in other countries. This requirement takes additional time and complicates the signing formalities.

If you have investigated other Living Will forms, the comprehensive Living Will form (with instructions) included in this book will appear to be overwhelming. But closer examination shows that much of the document consists of routine legal provisions which serve to reduce ambiguities and misunderstandings. There are only five or six major decisions that have to be made in filling out the form.

Because this book includes separate Living Will forms for each state (as of publication date there are forms for 41 states with Living Will statutes, plus common law forms for the other states), some readers will undoubtedly just sign the Living Will forms for their respective states.

If it is worth writing a Living Will at all, it is worth taking the time to write one that will remain valid in all situations. In order to make the process easier to understand, the legal and technical aspects have been simplified.

THE NON-LEGAL OBJECTIVES OF A LIVING WILL

A Living Will is a legal document and should be executed with all the formality and concern for exactness of language as any other legal document. At the same time, the declarant should remember that the Living Will is just as valuable as a medical directive committing the physicians and family to the desires of the patient.

It is difficult for family members to make the decision not to keep a relative alive through the use of modern technology despite the fact that the patient can not return to a meaningful life. Living Wills make this process easier by declaring what the patients would choose if they were able to do so themselves. It is easier to decide one's own fate than to decide the fate of others.

The fact that a patient has decided his or her own fate minimizes the guilt that loved ones frequently experience when they decide to stop therapy for a family member. Physicians also benefit from this guidance as they will not be confronted later with a claim of improper care. Without direction from the patient, standard medical care is directed toward maximum care in the maintenance of life. This philosophy is the doctor's creed in keeping with the medical ethics of the Hippocratic Oath.

The only principle that overrides this Oath is the wish of the patient as stated in the Living Will. The physician is obligated to honor these wishes. A Living Will also eases the physician's concern about the legal or professional repercussions of withholding or withdrawing care, which could result in a medical malpractice suit. Without this protection, doctors feel obliged to continue treatment whenever the patient is incapable of making that decision. Therefore, the Living Will takes out of the doctor's hands the decision-making process of whether to force the patient to live or allow the patient to die.

Writing a Living Will also gives the individual an ideal opportunity to initiate a discussion with his or her physician about issues involving "death with dignity." Such discussions are usually worthwhile and welcomed by both parties. The declarant would be able to find out whether the physician has moral objections to withholding or withdrawing therapy in specific situations. Such differences in philosophy can be discussed while the patient is mentally competent and understands the available options.

If conflicts of belief cannot be ironed out between patient and physician, the patient can select another physician **BEFORE** any such decision is necessary.

In drafting a Living Will, it is wise to remember that although these additional benefits may be as important as the legal benefits, the document should be legally binding. That is why the comprehensive Living Will declaration in this book is recommended over the typical short form Living Wills, which do not specifically address significant clinical situations and therefore fail to maintain the declarant's legal rights. Even if the directives in the comprehensive form are not immediately honored by health-care providers, they will serve as clear evidence of the patient's desires and will almost always be upheld by the courts.

Warning

Although Living Wills can serve to clarify a doctor-patient relationship, some physicians hold a well-founded resentment toward Living Wills. Cynics often mistakenly attribute this antagonism to the physician's (a) feeling of omnipotence or (b) lack of concern for patient's rights. This negative view of their concerns fails to take into consideration the physician's genuine belief that the Living Will documents frequently lead families and friends to put undue pressure on health-care givers to stop medical care—before it is appropriate to do so.

Friends and relatives of the patient are often unaware that the support systems which may be used unduly to prolong meaningless life are the same systems used to reverse imminent death and which could result in the patient returning to a high quality of life.

The procedure is not flawed. The situation in which the procedure begins or continues has flaws. Often relatives and friends equate the extent of the therapy with hopelessness. If a Living Will exists, they are upset when the physician refuses to stop treatment until proper evaluation has been completed and he or she decides whether or not the situation is hopeless.

The pressure to end treatment prematurely is inappropriate. The concept of the Living Will is based on the patient's right of *informed consent*, the right to decide whether to accept or forsake treatment with the full knowledge of the potential benefits or risks involved. It takes time to determine these benefits and risks, and it may require time before the medical evaluation can be undertaken.

Only when all the risks or benefits have been identified is it proper for the patient to decide whether to accept or refuse therapy. Similarly, only when this evaluation has been completed is it appropriate to follow the declarant's wishes as expressed in a Living Will.

THE LEGAL BASIS OF LIVING WILLS

Additive Bodies of Law

To understand the comprehensive Living Will form advocated in this book, the reader must appreciate that American law is comprised not of a single body of law but of a composite of two complementary sets of law.

The first type of law is called statutory law. It is the type of law that is produced by an act of a state or federal legislature and is written in very specific terms, which are entered (a process called "codification") into a series of books (called "statutes") of the state or federal government.

The second body of law is called the common law. This law is not written in specifics but arises out of court decisions handed down by judges after careful consideration of issues presented in specific cases. These decisions, which judges may base either on previous court decisions or on the interpretation of the constitution, are individually referred to as case law. When a number of cases considering a similar group of situations have been decided, a pattern emerges which is then collectively said to constitute common law.

An important part of the common law is a principle referred to as *stares decisis*. This principle states that once a situation has been considered and decided in one court, other courts in the same court system (or "jurisdiction"), when faced with the same type of situation, should make new decisions in keeping with the former decision. Because of this principle, a pattern tends to emerge within each state or federal court circuit (a circuit is a court which sits in two or more places within one judicial district) which can then be said to constitute the common law of that jurisdiction.

Statutory law is particularly needed when certainty of the law is more important than flexibility, as when dealing with criminal laws and such business matters as taxes, bankruptcy, and environmental protection. In contrast, common law is usually the more important in most civil matters because it gives the flexibility needed to deal with new situations as they arise and to tailor the law to individual needs.

A major difference between statutory law and the common law is the fact that the statutory law can only be changed in a prospective manner. To change statutory law requires a new act of the legislature, while courts have the ability to change the common law retroactively through a process called "overruling" the previous decision. It is contrary to the principle of *stares decisis* and is uncommon, but, because it can happen, the common law can not be looked on with the same certainty as statutory law.

In summary, statutory law has the advantage of being definite but has disadvantages in that it only applies to situations which have been specifically addressed by previous legislative acts. In contrast, common law has the advantage of being applicable to all situations but has the disadvantage of being somewhat indefinite. This means that a Living Will conforming to the wording of a statute can be considered legally binding, while the certainty of a common law Living Will is not as clear and the term legally binding is not appropriate.

Timing of Living Will Law

It was a quirk of timing that forced Living Will law to develop primarily as part of statutory law and not common law. The rights of individuals have traditionally developed under the common law because courts are better positioned to support the individual than are legislators, whose members must be reelected by a majority of the public. It is only when such rights become well accepted under the common law that attempts are usually made to codify these concepts into statutory law.

This process has not been dominant in Living Will law. The concept that an individual maintains the right of self-determination in health care *even after becoming incompetent* did not develop in the common law until after the Karen Quinlan decision in 1976. Unfortunately, at this time medical malpractice litigation was skyrocketing, especially in California. Because Living Will directives involve withholding or withdrawing treatment contrary to traditional medical standards of care, physicians were reluctant to honor such directives out of fear of involvement in a malpractice suit.

In an attempt to help physicians overcome this fear and comply with Living Will directives, California passed the first Living Will statute. The intent of the statute was to provide health-care givers with guaranteed immunity from malpractice suits and claims of unprofessional conduct for honoring Living Wills. Only the certainty provided by statutory law could accomplish the goal.

This premature emphasis on statutory Living Wills as opposed to common law Living Wills has been unfortunate because legislatures are reluctant to anger any of their constituency to develop broadly civil rights law. Legislators are reluctant to act despite the fact that common law has expanded the rights of individuals to control their own health care through Living Wills. Statutory law, in most states, has undergone few revisions incorporating these expanded rights into their original, narrowly defined language.

Therefore, it is not surprising that it is still the common law which provides the legal basis for most clinically significant Living Will declarations. In the forty plus states which have passed Living Will legislation, most physicians and attorneys, as well as the public, believe that these statutory acts contain all the individual's rights to refuse medical care. In fact these laws only grant very narrowly based rights compared to the much more expansive rights now recognized under common law.

Priority and Precedence

The development of common law rights is important to understanding Living Wills. To understand this process, we must examine the two closely related common law principles of "priority" and "precedence." "Priority" refers to the fact that some previous court decisions are more important than others in determining how courts should rule on an issue. Some courts have higher authority than others, and this priority is determined by the relationship the various U.S. courts have to each other.

The highest priority over all jurisdictions is given to decisions of the U.S. Supreme Court. When such decisions are in conflict with the decisions of any other court in the land, rulings of the U.S. Supreme Court overturn the common law which has been developed by previous lower court decisions. All further decisions of the lower courts must thereafter comply with those of the U.S. Supreme Court.

Below the U.S. Supreme Court, the American court system is divided into 50 state court systems plus a federal system, which is divided into 11 circuits plus one for the District of Columbia. Thus, there are at least 62 jurisdictions, plus those in the territories, each with its own individual body of common law.

Most states have three levels of courts, all of which are below the U.S. Supreme Court:

1. A trial court (lowest state court)
2. An appellate court
3. A state supreme court (highest state court)

The federal court system has only two levels of courts, which are below the U.S. Supreme Court:

1. The district courts in which trials are held
2. The circuit courts which hear appeals

The concept of priority says that within a jurisdiction, the higher the court making a decision and the more recent the decision, the greater its importance in future decisions. Priority, however, only applies within a single jurisdiction. The decision of a lower court in one jurisdiction can set the prevailing law in that jurisdiction even though the common law in most other jurisdictions based on higher court decisions would hold. For example, a court decision in the lower court in Michigan becomes the prevailing law in that jurisdiction even though the New York Supreme Court might rule otherwise.

"Precedence" is closely related to "priority" but encompasses the idea that well-reasoned decisions in other jurisdictions can also be influential in how a court should decide on a specific issue. Such decisions are said to give "precedence" for the court deciding on that issue. Such outside precedence is extremely important when the specific issue has never been addressed by a higher court within the same jurisdiction.

Priority is important when the issues are relatively simple and there are many written court decisions to consider within the jurisdiction. Precedence is important when the issues are complicated and there are few or no court decisions within the jurisdiction to consider in trying to determine the law.

The idea of Living Wills is too new for there to have been enough appellate court decisions on the various issues in each jurisdiction to determine how a lower court would rule. While there are over 60 jurisdictions and innumerable issues to be considered, there have been only some 100 court decisions which can be looked at for guidance. Consideration of case decisions within a home jurisdiction under the concept of priority is therefore inapplicable.

Fortunately, this is not required, for priority has not been followed by most states when dealing with issues of "death with dignity." Instead, state courts have relied heavily on precedents set by decisions reached by the Supreme Courts of

other states, most notably those of New Jersey, Massachusetts, New York, California, Illinois, and Florida. This process has been made possible by the concern, time, and effort taken by the Supreme Courts of these states in writing well-thought-out decisions that broadly protect the rights of the individual to self-determination in health care.

As a result, it becomes fairly safe to predict that if these jurisdictions are in agreement about the handling of various issues, it is unlikely that the courts in other states would decide differently. Only when there is conflict does it become hard to predict how a state court in another state is likely to rule.

SPECIAL NOTE

As stated earlier, the U.S. Supreme Court by avoiding the major issues that could have been addressed in the 1990 case of *Cruzan v Director, Missouri Department of Health* chose not to simplify this whole area of law. Thus all future decision making was placed back into the jurisdictions of the various states, presumably to avoid deciding on issues prematurely before they had been adequately addressed in the various courts of the land.

The Basis of Common Law Living Wills

Common law Living Wills first appeared in the 1970s as an outgrowth of the legal acceptance of the individual's right to self-determination in health care. They are still the only Living Wills in Massachusetts, Michigan, Nebraska, New York, Ohio, Pennsylvania, and Rhode Island.

Although it is difficult to believe that this right of self-determination is of recent origin, it is legally quite new. Many rights receive legal recognition only when a need appears. This right to control medical care after incompetency sets in came into existence in the 1960s after medicine developed the ability to extend meaningless life for prolonged periods.

Typical of common law, once the need for such a right developed, judges "created" the right out of previous law. In this case, the right was created from the previously recognized rights of informed consent and privacy. Under the right of informed consent, a patient is entitled to medical information before making a decision about proposed health care. Based on this right, courts have reasoned that the patient must then also have the right to decline care or the right to be informed would be meaningless.

Alternatively, some courts have found a right of self-determination in health care began with the so-called "right to privacy." This right itself was reasonably new, being first envisioned by the U.S. Supreme Court under the federal constitution in the 1963 decision, *Griswold* v *Connecticut*, and more specifically, appearing in the constitution in many states.

Living Wills: Validity, Legal Status, Significance

People frequently question whether Living Wills are (1) valid, (2) legally binding, or (3) clinically significant. Few differentiate between all three.

As discussed above, the only Living Wills that can be considered to be legally binding are those which (a) follow the wording requirements of the statute in the jurisdiction in which the declarant is receiving treatment and (b) are appropriately executed. Even if both these conditions exist, a Living Will is legally binding only if the existing clinical situation falls squarely within the narrow limits of the statute. These conditions make Living Wills legally binding primarily in situations where they are not needed and leave the clinically relevant situations largely uncovered.

As to validity, unless revoked, a Living Will is always valid as an expression of the declarant's desires. As common law broadly recognizes the

right of self-determination in health care, Living Wills that clearly express the declarant's desires are almost certain to determine the eventual care received—even if they are not initially thought to be binding by health-care providers. A properly written, common law Living Will that addresses an existing clinical situation has great significance not only socially but also legally. The limiting factor in the usefulness of Living Wills is seldom its legal status. It is the absence of a document covering the clinical situation at hand.

Even if the physician treating a patient feels a Living Will is not legally binding, it still maintains legal significance. If the health-care providers fail to accept and honor the directives as legally binding, the worst outcome will be the need for a judicial hearing; the "clear and convincing" evidence of the patient's desires provided by a valid Living Will should then determine the court's ruling.

When patients are terminally ill and suffering, time is of the essence and the requirement for a judicial hearing should be avoided if at all possible. In contrast, when dealing with a patient who is permanently unconscious or suffering from a slowly progressive disease, the added time of court involvement is much less significant. What is important is that the Living Will be valid and specific enough to give "clear and convincing" evidence of the patient's desires under the circumstances. If such information is provided in the document, one way or another the Living Will directives will eventually determine how the patient is treated.

Section Three

LEGAL BACKGROUND: STATUTORY LIVING WILLS

The comprehensive Living Will form suggested in this book expands the declarant's right of self-determination in health care to cover many of the clinical situations excluded by most Living Will statutes. It does so by incorporating accepted common law principles into the provisions of the Living Will form.

To explain the legal basis of the comprehensive Living Will form, this section will examine Living Will statutes in general and the Uniform Rights of the Terminally Ill Act in particular. This Act is a proposed universal Living Will statute which has now been adopted by approximately eight states. It will be analyzed not because it is the best, but because its provisions are probably the most widely used in Living Will statutes. Section Four will discuss the common law principles which have been integrated into the comprehensive Living Will form.

The information included in Sections Three, Four, and Five is not necessary in order to execute the Living Will form included in this book. Comments and directions related to the form itself are included in Section Five so there is no need to understand fully these chapters to execute the document. Readers who wish to prepare a significant Living Will document but are not interested in understanding the legal background should skip to Section Six for instructions on filling out the proposed comprehensive Living Will form.

LIVING WILL STATUTES: THE BASIC MECHANICS

A typical Living Will statute includes the following:

Legislative Declaration or Legislative Intent

This preliminary statement gives the reasons why the legislature believed a Living Will statute was advisable. Because it is not considered an operative part of the statute, it is omitted in many states. This omission is unfortunate because legislative intent can be instructive to courts deciding the meaning of an ambiguous provision in the statute or in expanding the statutory rights of the individual when making decisions.

A List of Definitions

This list is extremely important in Living Will statutes because the way in which terms are defined controls what clinical situations are covered under the statute and what therapy can be declined by the declarant. The most important of these definitions are those which define (a) terminal condition, illness, or disease and (b) life-support systems, or life-preserving procedures, or life-sustaining treatments. All three terms in both (a) and (b) are used in various state statutes but have essentially the same meaning.

A Proposed Living Will Form Declaration

In some states this form may be altered by the declarant, but in others it must be signed essentially as written. These form declarations are frequently made available in doctors' offices or attorneys' offices by professionals who lack sufficient time or expertise in the area of Living Wills to guide a client in writing a clinically significant Living Will document.

Directions for Execution

These directions include instructions about who may sign as witnesses of the declarant's signature, how many witnesses are needed, and whether the document must also be signed by a notary public. These directions also include how and whether a physician must be notified of the existence and contents of the Living Will and usually require the physician to make a copy a part of the patient's medical records.

What Activates the Living Will?

To activate a Living Will the attending physician, with or without confirmation from other physicians, must certify that the declarant (a) is incompetent and (b) is suffering from a terminal condition as defined in the statute. Such a patient is then referred to as a "Qualified Patient."

Requirements for Honoring Directives

A separate provision in the statute usually requires that once the declarant is certified as a qualified patient, then the health-care providers, be they physicians or hospitals, must honor the directives in the Living Will. If unable to do so for personal reasons, the doctor or hospital must transfer the patient to another physician or facility that is willing to follow the declarant's wishes.

Penalties for Failure to Honor Directives

A provision is usually included in the Living Will statute which is intended to force the physician and the medical facility to honor the declarant's directives. Although the provision may include potential fines or professional censure, it is more a threat than a reality. Physicians are never actually punished for failing to honor these directives.

Immunity of Health-Care Givers

All Living Will statutes contain provisions which protect health-care givers and make them immune from legal or professional repercussions for honoring declarant's directives. This provision is the major advantage of Living Wills based on statutes. Even though common law also provides immunity for health-care givers, physicians may

feel too uncertain of such immunity to honor common law directives. The problem arises, for example, if the statute lists six qualifying illnesses and the patient comes down with a serious but unlisted major illness. This problem is significant in the comprehensive Living Will and is the reason for repeated warnings throughout this text that a court hearing may be necessary before the Living Will will be honored if the declarant does not suffer from a qualifying disease under the state statute.

Designation of Health-Care Proxies

Frequently, Living Will statutes provide a method by which the declarants can (but need not) name other people to act on their behalf when they are not capable of acting for themselves. If this is done in what is called a "durable power of attorney for health care," more of the responsibility for decision making may be transferred to the designated person than is maintained by declarants themselves. If a declarant names another person to act on his or her behalf in the form of a "designated health-care proxy," the proxy's proper role is to insure that the directives in the declarant's Living Will are followed. The proxy will also help decide any ambiguities which may crop up from the wording of the declaration and deal with unanticipated situations.*

Standard Provisions

Most statutes include a series of standard provisions similar to those included in the Uniform Statute discussed below which relate to pregnancy, insurance, euthanasia, validity in other states, and so on.

GENERAL PROBLEMS WITH LIVING WILL STATUTES

Living Will statutes may appear to protect the individual's right of self-determination in health care, but on closer scrutiny, they are usually limited in their legal effect. This results from the

---

* NOTE: People who are designated health-care proxies and people who have powers of attorney for health care may be granted different powers in different states. Please check as the differences discussed here may not be applicable in your jurisdiction.

narrowness of definitions, ambiguity of language, and unwarranted exceptions placed in the law by legislators who are overly cautious and conservative in their approach and insist on "safeguards."

Usually the most important of these limiting factors is a definition of "terminal condition" or "terminal disease" which includes an estimated range of time during which the patient is expected to die. This may be legally convenient, but does not match the declarant's usual concept of a terminal condition as one which prevents the patient from ever recovering and returning to a meaningful life regardless of how long the heart may be kept beating.

In some states, "terminal condition" is so narrowly defined as to require that death be imminent, even if doctors use a treatment which the declarant wants withheld or withdrawn. In this case the reason for the statute altogether is nullified. If the declarant is expected to die quickly in spite of the treatment, there is no significant benefit in trying to avoid the treatment.

The other common way in which statutes limit the use of Living Wills is by failing to allow the declarant to authorize the withholding or withdrawing of surgery, medication, testing, and artificially administered nutrition and hydration. Most declarants find these interventions as unwarranted as mechanical life-support systems, but the statutes fail to do so. These and other undue limitations are dealt with extensively in the comprehensive Living Will form.

Subsection to Three

THE UNIFORM RIGHTS OF THE TERMINALLY ILL ACT

Because variation in law between the states causes problems for attorneys, travelers, and people who move, a legal committee, the Committee of Uniform Acts, is authorized to develop proposed uniform statutes for adoption by the various states in the hope of reducing conflicts of law. In 1985 this committee formulated the Uniform Rights of the Terminally Ill Act, usually referred to by its acronym URTIA, in an attempt to produce uniformity in Living Will statutes. To date Alaska, Arkansas, Iowa, Maine, Missouri, Montana, Nevada, North Dakota, and Oklahoma have passed acts based on its provisions.

Although URTIA was revised in 1989, it has been criticized more than most other proposed uniform acts. Except in the absence of legislative intent, it is nonetheless fairly representative of most Living Will statutes.

As URTIA is relatively short, it is included in its entirety below as an example of a typical Living Will statute. Comments directed at URTIA are also likely to be relevant to most other Living Will statutes. Because URTIA does not include a legislative intent, the California legislative intent (from the original Living Will statute) was included (see page 13) to help complete the example of a typical Living Will statute.

COMMENT ON LEGISLATIVE INTENT

Because California was the first state to pass a Living Will statute, most other states adopted modifications of this statement when they choose to include such a statement of intent. Although not stated in a way to define statutory law, such statements of intent may be referred to by courts in interpreting the provisions of the act and therefore do have an effect under common law.

URTIA DEFINITIONS

(1) "Attending physician" means the physician who has primary responsibility for the treatment and care of the patient.

(2) "Declaration" means a writing executed in accordance with the requirements of Section 2(a).

(3) "Health-care provider" means a person who is licensed, certified, or otherwise authorized by the law of this State to administer health care in the ordinary course of business or practice of the profession.

(4) "Life-sustaining treatment" means any medical procedure or intervention that, when administered to a qualified patient, will serve only to prolong the process of dying.

(5) "Person" means an individual, corporation, business trust, estate, trust, partnership, association, joint venture, government, governmental subdivision or agency, or any other legal or commercial entity.

(6) "Physician" means an individual licensed to practice medicine in this state.

(7) "Qualified patient" means a patient (18) or more years of age who has executed a declaration and who has been determined by the attending physician to be in a terminal condition.

(8) "State" means a State of the United States, the District of Columbia, the Commonwealth of Puerto Rico, or a territory or insular possession subject to the jurisdiction of the United States.

(9) "Terminal condition" means an incurable and irreversible condition that, without the administration of life-sustaining treatment, will, in the opinion of the attending physician, result in death within a relatively short time.

Comments on URTIA 1: Definitions

Three of these definitions not only define terms in the statute but are also what is legally called "substantive" in that they determine how the statute operates.

Suppose a declarant stipulates that he or she does not wish to be kept alive on life-sustaining treatment.

First, what is the definition of "life-sustaining treatment"? Undefined, any kind of treatment can be covered by the declaration. However, to be considered life-sustaining the treatment must "serve only to prolong the process of dying." This definition is problematic because most treatments serve multiple purposes; besides prolonging the process of dying, treatments may provide nutrition, or treat infection, or supply oxygen to the body tissues.

For example, in a person in a persistent vegetative state (as in the case of Karen Quinlan) the nutrition by artificial means maintains weight and sustains life as well as prolongs the dying process. This situation does not benefit the patient. To relieve this ambiguity, the comprehensive Living Will does not rely on a general definition but specifically indicates what therapies the declarant wants to forsake.

Second, what is the definition of "qualified patient"? Is the only qualified patient one who has executed a Living Will? If so, this definition fails to preserve the rights of individuals who have not executed Living Wills. To avoid this problem, many states permit physicians to certify a "qualified patient" even in the absence of a Living Will. This then triggers the possibility of an alternative legal means to avoid unwarranted therapy.*

Third, the term "terminal condition" requires that the patient, without treatment, be expected to die "within a relatively short time." Unfortunately, this definition excludes the approximately 10,000 living patients in the United States who, like Karen Quinlan and Nancy Cruzan in the past, are in a persistent vegetative state (discussed below), who will never regain consciousness, but who can live many years fed and hydrated by artificial means.

The term "terminal condition" also excludes patients who have other conditions which are not rapidly fatal but which make life so unbearable it is reasonable for patients to refuse to be treated if they so desire. Such conditions are dealt with extensively in the comprehensive Living Will form.

URTIA 2: DECLARATION RELATING TO USE OF LIFE-SUSTAINING TREATMENT

(a) An individual of sound mind and (18) or more years of age may execute at any time a declaration governing the withholding or withdrawal of life-sustaining treatment. The declarant may designate another individual of sound mind and (18) or more years of age to make decisions governing the withholding or withdrawal of life-sustaining treatment. The declaration must be signed by the declarant, or another individual at the declarant's direction, and witnessed by two individuals.

(b) A declaration directing a physician to withhold or withdraw life-sustaining treatment may (but need not be) in the following form:

Declaration

If I should have an incurable and irreversible condition that, without the administration of life-sustaining treatment, will, in the opinion of my attending physician, cause my death within a relatively short time, and I am no longer able to make decisions regarding my medical treatment, I direct my attending physician pursuant to the URTIA of this state to withhold or withdraw treatment that only prolongs the process of dying and is not necessary for my comfort or to alleviate pain.

Signed this _____ day of _____, _____.

Signature _____

Address _____

The declarant voluntarily signed this writing in my presence.

Witness _____

Address _____

Witness _____

Address _____

(c) A declaration that designates another individual to make decisions governing the withholding or withdrawal of life-sustaining treatment may (but need not be) in the following form:

* NOTE: Although called a Living Will statute, many states also include provisions as to how the rights of self-determination can be preserved in patients without Living Wills.

Declaration

If I should have an incurable and irreversible condition that, without the administration of life-sustaining treatment, will, in the opinion of my attending physician, cause my death within a relatively short time, and I am no longer able to make decisions regarding my medical treatment, I, _____, appoint _____ or, if he or she is not reasonably available or is unwilling to serve, _____, to make decisions on my behalf regarding withholding or withdrawal of treatment that only prolongs the process of dying and is not necessary for my comfort or to alleviate pain, pursuant to the Uniform Rights of the Terminally Ill Act of this State.

(If the individual[s] I have so appointed is [are] not reasonably available or is [are] unwilling to serve, I direct my attending physician, pursuant to the URTIA of this State, to withhold or withdraw treatment that only prolongs the process of dying and is not necessary for my comfort or to alleviate pain.)*

Signed this _____ day of _____, _____.

Signature _____

Address _____

The declarant voluntarily signed this writing in my presence.

Witness _____

Address _____

Witness _____

Address _____

Name and address of designee(s).

Name _____

Address _____

(d) The designation of an attorney-in-fact (pursuant to the Uniform Durable Power of Attorney Act or the Model Health-Care Consent Act), or the judicial appointment of an individual (guardian) who is authorized to make decisions regarding the withholding or the withdrawal of life-sustaining treatment, constitutes for purposes of this Act a declaration designating another individual to act for the declarant pursuant to subsection (a).

(e) A physician or other health-care provider who is furnished a copy of the declaration shall make it a part of the declarant's medical record and, if unwilling to comply with the declaration, promptly so advise the declarant and any individual designated to act for the declarant.

Comments on URTIA 2: Declaration Relating to Use of Life-Sustaining Treatment

The signing formalities in URTIA are extremely simple compared to most states and the form suggested in this book. Similarly, there is a minimal formality required in allowing a declarant to make oral declaration to be signed by another person.

(a) Almost all Living Will statutes, like URTIA, only allow adults to make declarations. Like URTIA, approximately one-third of the states now specifically authorize the designation of a health-care proxy to speak for the declarant as part of the Living Will declaration. An additional one-third allow for the naming of an agent of power of attorney for health care, independent of the Living Will document, while some states allow either. The exact duties and rights of such proxies vary significantly from state to state.

(b) URTIA allows substitution for the form declaration, but many states do not. Allowing substituted forms gives the declarant more discretion, which is appropriate, but makes it more difficult for a physician to know that he or she can honor the directives without fear of doing something illegal. Note that the declaration requires the continuation of comfort care as well as treatment of pain. This requirement for comfort care can cause difficulties, as discussed below.

(c) Note that the designation of a proxy in this form only covers situations in which the declarant is expected to die within a relatively short time and that comfort care is still required. Proxies are particularly helpful in dealing with situations which are not adequately covered by the Living Will directives, but these limitations can negate much of this desired effect.

(d) This worthwhile provision, unlike most Living Will statutes, requires the physician to read any Living Will declaration and advise the declarant if he or she is unwilling to comply. By so requiring, URTIA forces a physician who is reluctant to honor a patient's directives to discuss this problem with the patient prior to a situation of

---

* Strike out parenthetical language if you do not desire it.

conflict arising. In most cases, differences of opinion will be resolved. If not, the declarant has the opportunity to change attending physicians.

URTIA 3: WHEN A DECLARATION BECOMES OPERATIVE

A declaration becomes operative when (a) it is communicated to the attending physician and (b) the declarant is determined by the attending physician to be in a terminal condition and no longer able to make decisions regarding administration of life-sustaining treatment. When the declaration becomes operative, attending physician and other health-care providers shall act in accordance with its provisions and the instructions of a designee under Section 2(a) or comply with transfer requirements of Section 8.

Comment on URTIA 3: When a Declaration Becomes Operative

This provision is typical of most Living Will statutes, except that it combines many steps into a single provision. In keeping with the minimal requirement approach of URTIA, there are no specific requirements regarding how, when, or by whom the presence of a Living Will shall be communicated to the attending physician as required in some states. Note that URTIA clearly states that it is the physician who decides whether the patient is competent to make decisions. This requirement is in keeping with other Living Will statutes but is contrary to the usual legal determination of competency which is determined by a court.

URTIA 4: REVOCATION OF DECLARATION

(a) A declarant may revoke a declaration at any time and in any manner, without regard to the declarant's mental or physical condition. A revocation is effective upon its communication to the attending physician or other health-care provider by the declarant or a witness to the revocation.
(b) The attending physician or other health-care provider shall make the revocation a part of the declarant's medical record.

Comments on URTIA 4: Revocation of Declaration

This procedure for revocation is again in keeping with the very simple approach to formalities throughout URTIA but leaves open undesirable possibilities. The most important of these is the possibility that any relative who fails to agree with the declarant's beliefs about "death with dignity" could claim, after the declarant is incompetent, that the declarant has revoked his or her Living Will.

Another problem is that URTIA does not address the common situation in which the patient's attending physician changes, the primary care physician who attends the patient during periods of relative health having been replaced by the specialist who attends when the patient is critically ill.

These problems are addressed in the comprehensive Living Will form by limiting the number of people who can claim the Living Will has been revoked, by requiring the defacing of the original Living Will (not just a copy) to revoke the document, and by providing means by which the attending physician in a critical situation is given notice of the revocation of the Living Will document.

URTIA 5: RECORDING DETERMINATION OF TERMINAL CONDITION AND DECLARATION

Upon determination that a declarant is in a terminal condition, the attending physician who knows of a declaration shall record the determination and the terms of the declaration in the declarant's medical record.

Comment on URTIA 5: Recording Determination of Terminal Condition and Declaration

This is a standard provision in a Living Will statute. Some statutes additionally require that the physician also certify in the records that the patient is incompetent, while others require agreement by another physician who must also certify in the records that the patient is incompetent and terminal.

URTIA 6: TREATMENT OF QUALIFIED PATIENTS

(a) A qualified patient may make decisions regarding life-sustaining treatment as long as the patient is able to do so.

(b) This Act does not affect the responsibility of the attending physician or other health-care providers to provide treatment, including nutrition and hydration, for a patient's comfort care or alleviation of pain.

(c) Life-sustaining treatment must not be withheld or withdrawn pursuant to a declaration from an individual known to the attending physician to be pregnant as long as it is probable that the fetus will develop to the point of live birth with continued application of life-sustaining treatment.

Comments on URTIA 6: Treatment of Qualified Patients

Provision (a) is seldom seen in Living Will statutes and specifically directs that the patient's present decisions overrule any previously made directives in a Living Will. It purposely omits any mention of competency, giving the decision of an incompetent patient precedence over a directive written when the very same patient was fully competent. This provision is in keeping with the belief of most commentators (including the author) and the common law that when there is a question, a physician should protect the sanctity of life.

Normally, an incompetent individual cannot revoke a legal declaration made when competent. However, this is an established exception. It is interesting to consider the alternative possibility of an incompetent patient who asks that therapy be discontinued after signing a declaration requesting maximum care when competent. Which directive should then control? In this case, certainly the one made while the patient was competent.

Provision (b) is in conflict with common law which almost universally accepts the concept that nutrition and hydration is not required for patient comfort and should be considered no different from the withdrawal of other therapeutic modalities. Some of the newer Living Will statutes specifically recognize the right of the declarant to direct the discontinuation of nutrition and

hydration, but most continue to require the maintenance of nutrition by artificial means.

The URTIA provision (c) regarding pregnancy is very progressive compared to most Living Will statutes which void the declaration during pregnancy. Some critics say even this provision impinges on the rights of women to control their own medical care, but it is probably as good a compromise as will be accepted by the legal system.

URTIA 7: CONSENT BY OTHERS TO WITHDRAWAL OR WITHHOLDING OF TREATMENT

(a) If written consent to the withholding or withdrawal of treatment, witnessed by two individuals, is given to the attending physician, the attending physician may withhold or withdraw life-sustaining treatment from an individual who:

(i) has been determined by the attending physician to be in a terminal condition and no longer able to make decisions regarding administration of life-sustaining treatment;

(ii) has no effective declaration.

(b) The authority to consent or to withhold consent under the subsection (a) may be exercised by the following individuals, in order of priority:

(i) the spouse of the individual;

(ii) an adult child of the individual or, if there is more than one adult child, a majority of the adult children who are reasonably available for consultation;

(iii) the parents of the individual;

(iv) an adult sibling of the individual or, if there is more than one adult sibling, a majority of the adult siblings who are reasonably available for consultation; or,

(v) the nearest other adult relative of the individual by blood or adoption who is reasonably available for consultation.

(c) If a class entitled to decide whether to consent is not reasonably available for consultation and competent to decide, or declines to decide, the next class is authorized to decide, but an equal division in a class does not authorize the next class to decide.

(d) A decision to grant or withhold consent must be made in good faith. A consent is not valid if it conflicts with the expressed intention of the individual.

(e) A decision of the attending physician, acting in good faith that a consent is valid or invalid, is conclusive.

(f) Life-sustaining treatment must not be withheld or withdrawn pursuant to this section from a woman known by the attending physician to be pregnant as long as it is probable that the fetus will develop to the point of live birth with continued application of life-sustaining treatment.

Comments on URTIA 7: Consent by Others to Withdrawal or Withholding of Treatment

This section pertains to patients without Living Wills and is therefore not relevant to the concepts developed in this book, but it is of historical interest because of its relationship to the famous recent U.S. Supreme Court decision, *Cruzan* v *Director, Missouri Department of Health.*

Missouri has adopted URTIA as its basic Living Will statute, but, like most states, has not adopted it totally. This section, which was added to URTIA in 1989, has not been adopted by Missouri. In its absence, there was no statutory procedure for Nancy Cruzan, who had been unresponsive for four years, to exercise her right of self-determination in health care through the wishes of her parents. Her parents therefore had to rely on Missouri common law, which did not permit the discontinuation of care without "clear and convincing" evidence of what Nancy herself would desire. As there was no Living Will and the courts failed to find "clear and convincing" evidence of Nancy's desires, the court ruled that she had to be given nutrition by artifical means, even though everyone accepted the fact that Nancy would always remain unresponsive. If she had executed a Living Will or if this provision existed in the Missouri code, the outcome would undoubtedly have been different.*

Note that there is still a procedural flaw in the URTIA plan. Assume that a patient has an incurable and irreversible disease such as lung cancer. Assume further that after a test is done to check progress of the cancer the patient has trouble breathing and must be put on a respirator temporarily. Assume further that the patient would want this treatment temporarily but has not expressed this wish, and that both the spouse and the physi-

cian believe, in good faith, that temporary treatment will only lead to greater discomfort for the patient. Under URTIA, the spouse has the power to direct that the respirator not be employed. The spouse need only sign such a directive and have it witnessed by two other individuals. In this case such power is contrary to the patient's right of self-determination in health care.**

URTIA 8: TRANSFER OF PATIENTS

An attending physician or other health-care provider who is unwilling to comply with the Act shall take all reasonable steps as promptly as practicable to transfer care of the declarant to another physician or health-care provider who is willing to comply.

Comment on URTIA 8: Transfer of Patients

URTIA has been criticized for not doing more to insure that patient care is quickly transferred if the physician does not honor the directive. Whether greater penalties for failing to honor the directives would have any effect is questionable. A better method of insuring that directives are honored is to designate a health-care proxy who has the authority to transfer the patient's care to that of another physician if it is required.

URTIA 9: IMMUNITIES

(a) A physician, or health-care provider, is not subject to civil or criminal liability, or discipline for unprofessional conduct, for giving effect to a declaration or to the direction of an individual designated pursuant to Section 2(a) in the absence of knowledge of the revocation of a declaration, or for giving effect to a written consent under Section 7.

(b) A physician or other health-care provider, whose action under this Act is in accord with reasonable medical standards, is not subject to criminal or civil liability, or discipline for

---

* NOTE: Following the U.S. Supreme Court decision, based on additional information regarding Nancy Cruzan's desires, the Missouri court did permit the discontinuation of nutrition supplied by artificial means.

** This flaw occurs because URTIA, like other Living Will statutes, fails to specifically require the declarant's incapacity be irreversible before others make the decision to forgo care on the declarant's behalf.

unprofessional conduct, with respect to that action.

(c) A physician or other health-care provider, whose decision about the validity of consent under Section 7 [see pp. 28–29] is made in good faith, is not subject to criminal or civil liability, or discipline for unprofessional conduct, with respect to that decision.

(d) An individual designated pursuant to Section 2(a) [see p. 25] or an individual authorized to consent pursuant to Section 7 [see pp. 28–29], whose decision is made or consent is given in good faith pursuant to this Act is not subject to criminal or civil liability, or discipline for unprofessional conduct, with respect to that decision.

Comments on URTIA 9: Immunities

Provisions similar to these in Section 9 of URTIA appear in all Living Will statutes in order to promote physician compliance with advanced directives in a Living Will. Few are as extensive or as well written as the URTIA provisions. Although this provision does not appear to give similar protection to health-care facilities, it probably does because in most situations a corporation is legally considered a "person." As almost all health-care facilities are corporations, they probably would fall within the definition of a health-care provider as defined in URTIA.

The lack of immunity for honoring directives under a common law Living Will is one of the biggest problems to be overcome. Unlike most other statutory provisions, immunity can only be given by state legislatures. It cannot be provided for in the Living Will form. The comprehensive Living Will form attempts to give as much immunity to physicians and other health-care givers as possible, but declarants must expect some delay to result in honoring non-statutory directives because of the uncertainty they will cause for the medical profession.

URTIA 10: PENALTIES

(a) A physician or other health-care provider who willfully fails to transfer the care of a patient in accordance with Section 8 [see p. 29] is guilty of a [class _____ misdemeanor].

(b) A physician who willfully fails to record a determination of terminal condition or the terms of a declaration in accordance with Section 5 [see p. 27] is guilty of a [class _____ misdemeanor].

(c) An individual who willfully conceals, cancels, defaces, or obliterates the declaration of another individual without the declarant's consent or who falsifies or forges a revocation of the declaration of another individual is guilty of a [class _____ misdemeanor].

(d) An individual who falsifies or forges the declaration of another individual, or willfully conceals or withholds personal knowledge of a revocation under Section 4 [see p. 27], is guilty of a [class _____ misdemeanor].

(e) A person who requires or prohibits the execution of a declaration as a condition for being insured for, or receiving, health-care services is guilty of a [class _____ misdemeanor].

(f) A person who coerces or fraudulently induces an individual to execute a declaration is guilty of a [class _____ misdemeanor].

(g) The penalties provided in this section do not displace any sanction applicable under the law.

Comment on URTIA 10: Penalties

The proposed penalties in URTIA are similar to those in most Living Will statutes but more complete and better written. Provision (d), however, is in conflict with many state statutes which consider falsifying or forging a Living Will declaration or concealing a revocation to be a felony. While there may be some question as to the seriousness of so doing when dealing with patients who are incompetent and terminal, doing so with patients who have other chronic but non-terminal diseases should certainly be a felony.

URTIA 11: MISCELLANEOUS PROVISIONS

(a) Death resulting from the withholding or withdrawal of life-sustaining treatment in accordance with this Act does not constitute, for any purpose, a suicide or homicide.

(b) The making of a declaration pursuant to Section 2 [see pp. 25–26] does not affect the sale, procurement, or issuance of a policy of life insurance or annuity, nor does it affect, impair, or modify the terms of an existing policy of life insurance or annuity. A policy of life insurance or annuity is not legally impaired or invalidated by the withholding or withdrawal of life-sustaining treatment in the event of a terminal condition.

(c) A person may not prohibit or require the execution of a declaration as a condition for being insured for, or receiving, health-care services.

(d) This Act creates no presumption concerning the intention of an individual who has revoked or has not executed a declaration with respect to the use, withholding, or withdrawal of life-sustaining treatment in the event of a terminal condition.

(e) This Act does not affect the right of a patient to make decisions regarding use of life-sustaining treatment, as long as the patient is able to do so, or impair or supersede a right or responsibility that a person has to affect the withholding or withdrawal of medical care.

(f) This act does not require a physician or other health-care provider to take action contrary to reasonable medical standards.

(g) This act does not condone, authorize, or approve mercy killing or euthanasia.

Comments on URTIA 11: Miscellaneous Provisions

All of these provisions are included in almost all state statutes.

Provision (a) is included to protect health-care workers from being charged with homicide or assisted suicide (euthanasia) for honoring patient directives.

Provision (b) is included primarily to be sure there is no problem with an insurance company claiming they do not have to honor an insurance policy that excludes payments for homicide or suicide.

Provision (c) is intended to avoid a situation in which pressure to sign a Living Will declaration is placed on an individual by people who would benefit by limiting their financial exposure if the individual did so. A more difficult task concerns the problem of family coercion. It is hard to tell the difference between undue pressure from family members and the declarant's legitimate desire to limit depletion of family finances for an irreversible terminal illness. This area is one in which the Living Will does have a similarity to a regular

will. It should truly reflect only the personal desires of the declarant without outside influence. One advantage of including the pro-care option in a Living Will is that it promotes the idea that a request for all reasonable medical care to be given is also an appropriate response to any illness.

Provision (d) states that a person without a Living Will cannot be assumed to want all care. This provision is included to differentiate the Living Will from any other statutorily permitted instruments, such as a regular will, in the absence of which the law makes a presumption about what is desired. For instance, in the absence of a regular will, the law provides what is referred to as the "intestate rules of succession," which states how the assets are distributed under these circumstances.

Provision (e) is important for physicians because it gives them great discretionary power not to conform to directives they think are inappropriate. Although this provision is frequently criticized, when we consider how much we rely on physician discretion in medical care aimed at preserving life, it is not inappropriate to give them the same discretion to decide when the possibility of a return to meaningful life still exists.

URTIA 12: WHEN HEALTH-CARE PROVIDER MAY PRESUME VALIDITY OF DECLARATION

In the absence of knowledge to the contrary, a physician or other health-care provider may assume that a declaration complies with this Act and is valid.

Comment on URTIA 12: When Health-Care Provider May Presume Validity of Declaration

This provision is another provision highly supportive of the need to encourage physicians to honor patient directives.

URTIA 13: RECOGNITION OF DECLARATION EXECUTED IN ANOTHER STATE

A declaration executed in another state in compliance with the law of that state or of this state is valid for purposes of this Act.

Comment on URTIA 13: Recognition of Declaration Executed in Another State

Too few states presently have such provisions. In its absence, the common law basis of Living Wills still exists, but there is no reason why efforts should not be made to make Living Wills universally accepted.

URTIA 14: EFFECT OF PREVIOUS DECLARATION

An instrument executed anywhere before the effective date of this Act which substantially complies with Section 2(a) [see p. 25] is effective under the Act.

URTIA 15: UNIFORMITY OF APPLICATION AND CONSTRUCTION

This Act shall be applied and construed to effectuate its general purpose to make uniform the law with respect to the subject of this Act among states enacting it.

URTIA 16: SHORT TITLE

This Act may be cited as the Uniform Rights of the Terminally Ill Act (1989).

URTIA 17: SEVERABILITY CLAUSE

If any provision of this Act or its application to any person or circumstance is held invalid, the invalidity does not affect other provisions or application of this Act which can be given effect without the invalid provision or application, and to this end the provisions of this Act are severable.

Comment on URTIA 17: Severability Clause

This severability clause is a common provision in many legal contracts. In case any provision of the act is subsequently found to be invalid by a court, it does not end the validity of the entire act. A similar severability clause will be found in the comprehensive Living Will form which provides that if any directive is found to be invalid, it will not void the rest of the directives in the form.

URTIA 18: EFFECTIVE DATE

This Act takes effect on _____.

URTIA 19: REPEAL

The following acts and parts of acts are repealed*:
(1)
(2)
(3)

STATES WITHOUT STATUTES

In states without Living Will statutes, such as Massachusetts, Michigan, Nebraska, New York, Ohio, Pennsylvania, and Rhode Island, the legality of a Living Will declaration is based totally on common law. In this situation, the written document should include many of the provisions normally supplied by the statute.

Surprisingly, many supporters of "death with dignity" believe the absence of a statute is an advantage, not a disadvantage, for common law tends to be more protective of individual rights than does legislatively passed statutory law. This thinking reinforces the misconception that statutory law and common law are exclusive, not additive.

The preference for common law, not the lack of concern for individual rights, has led many large liberal states to refrain from passing Living Will legislation. Because drafters of Living Wills in these states are forced to address the various issues normally covered by statutes within individually written Living Will documents, more time may be spent in drafting with resultant improvement in the documents themselves.

* EDITOR'S NOTE: Each state, as it adopts URTIA, inserts its own dates and changes.

Section Four

BASIS OF LIVING WILL VALIDITY IN THE COMMON LAW

Approximately 100 case decisions which bear on the legality of Living Wills have now been published. (Not all legal decisions are published, especially those coming from the lower state courts.) A majority of these decisions are from courts in California, Florida, Massachusetts, New Jersey, and New York, but several influential cases have come from other jurisdictions.

All the cases discussed in this section appear in alphabetical order by abbreviated case designation in Section Eight. The list is included for curious readers and those professionals who might be interested in looking up the complete case in a legal library. Also included for curious readers is a discussion of some of the non-Living Will "death with dignity" issues which have been addressed in court decisions. Many of these have been decided differently in various jurisdictions or even by different courts within the same jurisdiction. When this situation has occurred, it is difficult to predict how the issue would have been decided in any particular court or court system. Luckily, these differences almost always relate to decision making in the absence of a Living Will, a condition the reader is seeking to avoid.

In contrast to the narrow interpretation of Living Will statutes, the case decisions based on common law have generally interpreted the rights of individuals to control their own health care broadly. This chapter summarizes the general common law principles that are supported by these decisions. Because these decisions only hold priority in the jurisdiction in which they were decided, they need not be followed in other jurisdictions. Even so, many of the principles

upon which these decisions are based have been so universally accepted that it is highly unlikely any other jurisdiction would decide against the precedence they set on the same issue.

PRINCIPLE 1: THE PATIENT HAS THE RIGHT OF SELF-DETERMINATION IN HEALTH CARE

The right of the individual to control his or her own medical care is now universally accepted. While the origin of this right has been variously ascribed to the common law right of informed consent or to the constitutional right of privacy under a state or federal constitution, the right is interpreted in the same way in all states.*

In expressing this right, most courts quote the following statement first articulated in 1891 by the U.S. Supreme Court in *Union Pacific Railway Co.* v *Botsford:*

> No right is held more sacred, or is more carefully guarded by the common law, than the right of every individual to the possession and control of his own person, free from all restraint or interference of others, unless by clear and unquestionable authority of the law.

Another quotation often referred to by the courts is the following, written by New York's famous Judge Benjamin Cardoza in 1914 in *Schloendorff* v *Society of New York Hospital:*

---

* NOTE: The Supreme Court in *Cruzan* found the same right as part of the individual's right to liberty.

Every human being of adult years and sound mind has a right to determine what shall be done with his own body.

This right of self-determination in health care applies even when the patient chooses to refuse therapy, which would be likely to save his or her life and without which he or she is likely to die.

Two well known cases that demonstrate this principle are *In re Quackenbush* (New Jersey) and *Lane* v *Candure* (Massachusetts), in both of which a patient was allowed to refuse amputation of the leg even though such refusal would cause overwhelming infection and death.

PRINCIPLE 2: THE RIGHT OF SELF-DETERMINATION IN HEALTH CARE IS BASED ON THE COMMON LAW RIGHT TO INFORMED CONSENT AND THE CONSTITUTIONAL RIGHT TO PRIVACY

In the Arizona case *Rasmussen* v *Fleming*, it was noted that the basis of the individual's right of self-determination in health care can stem from a (1) state or (2) federal constitutional right to privacy, or from the (3) common law right of informed consent. In *Rasmussen*, the court found all three rights applicable.

The following cases in the following states have also accepted this right to privacy under the federal constitution:

> *Bouvia* v *County of Riverside*, California
> *Brophy* v *New England Mount Sinai Hospital*, Massachusetts
> *In re Farrell*, New Jersey
> *Foody* v *Manchester Memorial Hospital*, Connecticut
> *In re Welfare of Colyer*, Washington
> *In re Severns*, Delaware
> *In re Spring*, Massachusetts
> *Leach* v *Akron General Medical Center*, Ohio
> *Satz* v *Perlmutter*, Florida
> *Superintendent of Belchertown State School* v *Saikewicz*, Massachusetts
> *In re Quinlan*, New Jersey
> *In re L.H.R.*, Georgia

But in *Cruzan* v *Harmon*, the Missouri court failed to find such a federal constitutional right.

Other state cases which have found such a right to privacy under the state constitution include:

> *Bouvia*, California
> *Guardianship of Barry*, Florida
> *Quinlan*, New Jersey
> *Colyer*, Washington
> *Corbett* v *D'Alessandro*, Florida

Cases which have found the right of self-determination under the common law right of informed consent include:

> *Brophy*, Massachusetts
> *Farrell*, New Jersey
> *Foody*, Connecticut
> *Colyer*, Washington
> *In re Conservatorship of Torres*, Minnesota
> *Delio* v *Westchester County Medical Center*, New York
> *In re Conroy*, New Jersey
> *Matter of Storar*, New York
> *Conservatorship of Drabick*, California
> *In re Gardner*, Maine
> *Saikewicz*, Massachusetts
> *In re Jobes*, New Jersey

PRINCIPLE 3: THE RIGHTS OF SELF-DETERMINATION IN HEALTH CARE DO NOT CEASE WHEN THE PATIENT BECOMES INCOMPETENT

It is now universally recognized that the right of self-determination in health care does not cease when a patient becomes mentally incompetent to make choices or physically unable to communicate his or her wishes. The question is how to determine those wishes, who is to make the decisions, and on what basis are the decisions to be made.

This principle was discussed in *Morgan* v *Olds*, which was decided in the Iowa court of appeals:

> Incompetency does not vitiate the patient's rights to choose the particular treatment or the doctor's duty to obtain the necessary consent. To preserve this right, a "substituted judgement" is made on the incompetent's behalf by a surrogate decision-maker. This decision is usually made by members of the incompetent's family. The deci-

sion made should, after considering the patient's actual interest, preferences, present and future incompetency, be the decision that would have been made by the patient if competent.

Some other case decisions which have expressed this opinion that the right of self-determination continues after the development of incompetency include:

Application of Eichner, New York
Quinlan and *Conroy*, New Jersey
Strachan v *John F. Kennedy Memorial Hospital*, New Jersey
Colyer, Washington
Severns, Delaware
Saikewicz, Massachusetts
Barry, Florida
Gardner, Maine
Leach, Ohio
Rasmussen, Arizona
Foody, Connecticut

No decisions have held otherwise.

The process by which the patient's right of self-determination in health care is continued beyond incompetency is referred to as "surrogate decision making" and the person who makes the decision, the "surrogate decision maker." A Living Will written when an individual is competent and free of stress, is the best way to tell the decision maker what the individual's desires would have been if he or she was still competent.

A second best method of preserving the patient's rights may be for the patient to designate a proxy health-care decision maker to speak on his or her behalf in the event that he or she becomes incompetent. In this case a Living Will does not exist, but, presumably, the person chosen would know the patient's views and would share a similar concept of life. Unfortunately, it is difficult for the decision maker not to project his or her own views on those of the patient. Because even the decision makers may be aware of this difficulty, they may waiver, afraid that they are making decisions for their own benefit, thus becoming inappropriate decision makers.

PRINCIPLE 4: THE RIGHT OF SELF-DETERMINATION IS NOT ABSOLUTE AND MUST BOW TO CERTAIN STATE INTERESTS

Just as all courts have now accepted the right of the individual to self-determination in health care and the preservation of this right when the patient becomes incompetent, it is also universally accepted that this right is not absolute and that the state has contrary interests which must be balanced against the individual's rights. The four state interests are:

1. The preservation of life.
2. The protection of interests of innocent third parties.
3. The prevention of suicide.
4. The maintenance of the ethical integrity of the medical profession.

This need to balance the right of self-determination against the state's interests was first stated in the famous *Quinlan* case:

We think that the State's interest *contra* weakens and the individual's right to privacy grows as the degree of bodily invasion increases and the prognosis dims. Ultimately there comes a point at which the individual's rights overcome the State interest.

This early reference to the concept of a need to balance the individual's rights against the four state interests has now been expanded and accepted in at least the following case decisions:

Rasmussen, Arizona
Conroy, New Jersey
Foody, Connecticut
Bartling v *Superior Court*, California
Colyer, Washington
Leach, Ohio
Satz, Florida
Saikewicz, Massachusetts
In re Boyd, District of Columbia
In re Estate of Longeway, Illinois
Gray v *Romeo*, District of Columbia and R.I.
State v *McAfee*, Georgia
Farrell, New Jersey
Spring, Massachusetts
Brophy, Massachusetts

Bouvia, California
John F. Kennedy Hospital v *Bludworth*, Florida
L.H.R., Georgia

No states have found to the contrary.

In spite of a need to balance the rights and interests between the individual and the state, it is only in extreme circumstances that courts have failed to rule in favor of the individual's rights over state interests when the individual's desires are clearly known. Such situations are not likely to be relevant in a situation in which a Living Will exists. A few of these unusual cases are discussed below in order to impress upon the reader the fact that courts only rule against the known desires of patients in most unusual circumstances.

The State's Interest in the Preservation of Life

While the state's interest in preserving life is said to be its most significant interest, it is seldom an issue dealing with Living Will problems. As stated in *Colyer*, the state's interest in preserving life weakens and must yield to the patient's interest where treatment at issue "serves only to prolong a life inflicted with an incurable condition." As these are the situations in which Living Will directives are relevant, the state's interest in preserving life can not prevail.

The situations in which this interest of the state in preserving life has been used by courts to overrule the right of self-determination have been limited. For instance, a court overruled a parent's refusal to allow blood transfusions for a child on religious grounds in the case of *Muhlenberg Hospital* v *Paterson, New Jersey*.

Similarly, in *Jefferson* v *Griffin-Spaulding County Hospital*, a Georgia court ordered a pregnant woman to undergo a Cesarean section over her religious objections when complications of pregnancy made this operation the only way to preserve the life of the unborn child, again referring to the state's interest in preserving life.

State Protection of Innocent Third Parties

Courts have occasionally refused to allow a patient to direct that medical care be discontinued when it would adversely affect an innocent third party. This situation most commonly occurs when an expectant mother refuses blood transfusion for religious reasons thereby threatening the life of an unborn child, as in *In re President & Directors of Georgetown College*.*

Such concern for an innocent third party may also occur when a single working parent would choose to end his or her life-support systems thereby eliminating their children's only financial support. For example, in *Indian River Memorial Hospital & Schlamowitz* v *Cochran*, a 48-year-old man was not allowed to refuse kidney dialysis because he was financially responsible for three dependents.

Although this interest in the welfare of third parties may control the right of pregnant women to direct the stopping of therapy, it is again not relevant to the unusual situation in which Living Wills are involved.

State's Interest in Preventing Suicide

On at least two occasions a court has refused a patient the right to refuse medical care on the grounds that it would constitute suicide. In *In re Caulk*, a New Hampshire state court had to decide whether to allow a prisoner to starve himself to death rather than live out a life sentence. The court ordered placement of a feeding tube saying that to honor the patient's request that no nutrition or hydration be given was contrary to the state's interest in preventing suicides.

In *In re Sanchez*, a New York court ordered hunger strikers to be fed against their will by artificial means.

This state interest in preventing suicide is the basis for the illegality of euthanasia, as stated in *Rasmussen*:

> For humane reasons, with informed consent, a physician may do what is medically necessary to alleviate severe pain, or cease to omit treatment to permit a terminally ill patient whose death is imminent (or who is in irreversible coma) to die. However, he should not intentionally cause death.

As noted above, this concern is specifically dealt with in most Living Will statutes by a provision that states that withholding or withdrawing

---

* EDITOR'S NOTE: Most courts have honored the woman's right to refuse transfusions in this situation.

care as directed in a Living Will document does not constitute suicide. This concept is also supported by common law.

State's Interest in Maintaining the Integrity of the Medical Profession

As the medical society moves toward greater acceptance of the rights of individuals to stop care when hope for a return to meaningful life is gone, the interest in safeguarding the integrity of the medical profession is seldom given as a reason for continuing care in patients against their directives. A court, however, may not honor a directive that would constitute a request for inappropriate medical care. For example, if a patient requests medical care for a bleeding ulcer and then refuses appropriate transfusions, the courts may take the view that these contrary actions constitute a request for care which imperils the integrity of the medical profession because it dictates the use of inappropriate care. This situation occurred in *Crouse-Irving Memorial Hospital* v *Paddock* (New York) and the similar case, *U.S.* v *George* (Connecticut), in which courts ordered necessary blood transfusions despite religious objections of patients after they requested medical care for themselves.

The above cases are the exceptions. In essentially all the other cases which are not included, courts have decided to uphold the directives of a competent patient to withhold care. Some of these cases will be discussed below, but it is evident that when the desires of the patient are known, it takes extraordinary circumstances for a court to refuse to honor those directives.

In discussing the place of the Living Will with respect to the balance between the rights of the individual and those of the state, the Missouri Supreme Court recently wrote in *Cruzan* v *Harmon*:

> The state's concern with the sanctity of life rests on the principle that life is precious and worthy of preservation without regard to its quality. This latter concern is especially important when concerning a person who has lost the ability to direct her medical treatment. . . . In response to the dilemmas which attend the increasing ability of medical science to maintain life, where death would have come quickly in former days, legislatures across the country adopted so-called

"Living Will" statutes. These permit a competent person to decree in a formal document that she would refuse death-prolonging medical treatment in the event of a terminal illness and an accompanying inability to refuse such treatment as a result of incompetency.

The U.S. Supreme Court expressed these sentiments in the now famous decision, *Cruzan* v *Director, Missouri Department of Health*, after it reviewed the original *Cruzan* v *Harmon* decision.

PRINCIPLE 5: A DECLARANT'S RIGHT OF SELF-DETERMINATION IN HEALTH CARE MAY BE PRECLUDED BY PREGNANCY

Many Living Will statutes prevent the withholding or withdrawing of life-support systems during pregnancy. These provisions have been challenged in commentaries on a number of occasions because they appear to be in direct conflict with freedom of choice granted by the U.S. Supreme Court in *Roe* v *Wade*, but no court decisions have been written addressing this issue. Each time the issue is raised, as it was in *Dinino* v *State*, the court has found a way not to decide.

Although the challenges to this exclusion have never resulted in a court decision, it is interesting to note that the Uniform Right of the Terminally Ill Act (URTIA) and some states now recognize a woman's right to direct the withholding or withdrawal of care through Living Wills in certain situations even if she is pregnant.

PRINCIPLE 6: THE COMMON LAW RIGHTS OF SELF-DETERMINATION IN HEALTH CARE ARE IN ADDITION TO THE RIGHTS UNDER A LIVING WILL STATUTE

Many states that have Living Will statutes specifically include in the statute a statement that the rights granted therein are in addition to and do not limit in any way the common law rights of the patient to control his or her own medical care. This statement means that Living Wills that are more comprehensive than the statutory declaration are also valid under common law, and that Living Wills written in other jurisdictions may be validated under the common law of the state in which the patient is being treated.

Even without such statutory statements, courts have repeatedly held that the common law basis for Living Wills exists independent of the rights granted by the statute. Provisions in a Living Will document which do not conform to the statute are still held as "clear and convincing" evidence of the patient's desires and are honored under the right of self-determination in health care unless contravened by one of the four state interests discussed above.

In a typical case, *Corbett*, which followed the passage of Florida's Living Will statute, the Second District Court of Florida held that a nasogastric feeding tube could be removed legally from a 75-year-old woman who had been in a persistent vegetative state for four years even though removal would result in her death. This action was ordered in spite of the fact that the permanent vegetative state could not be included under the definition of terminal disease in the Florida statute and the statute specifically precluded removal of nutrition by artificial support systems. In taking this action the court specifically referred to the Florida provision which provided that relief under the Life-Prolonging Procedure Act of Florida is to be added to relief already provided by common law and other statutes.

In another related case, *In re Prange*, a Living Will had been written but was not properly witnessed. Although this situation precluded withholding therapy under the statute, the court still found that the Living Will gave "clear and convincing" evidence of the patient's desires and permitted withholding of therapy under the common law rights of the patient.*

Similar statements have also been made by courts in Maine, Washington, and California.

PRINCIPLE 7: REMOVING A FEEDING TUBE USED TO GIVE NUTRITION AND HYDRATION IS NO DIFFERENT FROM STOPPING OTHER MEDICAL THERAPY

Some people feel that stopping nutrition and hydration is different than stopping other therapy because it results in death from starvation and dehydration as opposed to death from the patient's disease.

Courts, however, have routinely found to the contrary based on the best medical evidence and have held that the withholding or withdrawal of nutrition and hydration is not painful to the patient and is as natural a way for a disease to result in death as any other. Under the resulting common law, withdrawal of all forms of medical therapy is considered equal and directives that nutrition and hydration be stopped will be held valid if so specified in a Living Will.

This approach has been accepted in at least the following decisions and states:

Conroy, New Jersey
Gardner, Maine
In re Rodas, Colorado
McConnell v *Beverly Enterprises-*
  Connecticut, Inc, Connecticut (gastronomy tube only)
Brophy, Massachusetts
Corbett, Florida
Drabick, California
Rasmussen, Arizona
In re Guardianship of Grant, Washington

In contrast, a few state decisions, including:

*In re Westchester County Medical Center on
  Behalf of O'Conner*, New York
Cruzan v *Harmon*, Missouri
Longeway, Illinois

do not equate nutrition with other therapy, requiring clearer evidence of the declarant's desires when it comes to discontinuing nutrition than other procedures. All three, however, would allow discontinuation of such nutrition by artificial means if it was so directed in a Living Will.

PRINCIPLE 8: PATIENTS IN A PERSISTENT VEGETATIVE STATE CAN BE CONSIDERED TERMINAL

Most patients who are considered comatose after an accident or a medical catastrophe either regain consciousness or die within a relatively short period of time. Those who do not usually develop what is called a persistent vegetative state (PVS). A patient who is in a persistent vegetative state

---

* This decision was subsequently voided by an appeals court for other reasons, but still gives evidence of the thinking of courts in general.

does not need machines to help him or her breathe or maintain circulation. Also, the patient appears to go through sleep cycles and even to respond occasionally to outside stimuli, but he or she never truly relates to society. These patients can live for years given nutrition and hydration by artificial means without hope of ever returning to a meaningful life.

Because some patients in a coma regain consciousness early in the course of their condition, a person in a PVS cannot be judged to be medically terminal after a few weeks. However, when the PVS remains stable for many months, it is reasonable to assume that the condition is terminal.

The legal situation for patients in a PVS was discussed well in *Jobes*:

> [W]e find it difficult to conceive of a case in which the State could have an interest strong enough to subordinate a patient's right to choose not to be sustained in a persistent vegetative state.

Only the Arkansas Living Will statute presently accepts the persistent vegetative state as being included under its Living Will statute, but courts, beginning with *Quinlan*, have routinely considered patients who are in a persistent vegetative state for a long period of time to be terminal.*

Case decisions and states which have authorized discontinuation of life-support systems for patients in a PVS now include at least:

Barber Superior Court, California
Delio and *Eichner*, New York
In re Peter and *Jobes*, New Jersey
In re Guardianship of Hamlin, Washington
Romeo, Rhode Island
Torres, Minnesota
Brophy, Massachusetts
Gardner, Maine
Prange and *Longeway*, Illinois
L.H.R., Georgia
Corbett, Florida
Foody, Connecticut
Severns, Delaware
In re N., District of Columbia
Rasmussen, Arizona

None have refused to do so in the presence of "clear and convincing" evidence that it would be the patient's desire.

PRINCIPLE 9: THE RIGHT OF INCOMPETENT PATIENTS TO CONTROL THEIR OWN MEDICAL CARE THROUGH ADVANCED DIRECTIVES IS NOT LIMITED TO TERMINAL CONDITIONS

Living Wills and Living Will statutes typically deal with patients who will die over a relatively short period of time even with therapeutic intervention. But these are not the only people who are likely to benefit by advance directives because they are not the ones who are likely to be kept alive for long periods of time without potential benefit. Patients in the persistent vegetative state are much more likely than terminal patients to benefit by having executed a Living Will because they can live for many years in that condition.

The concept of the Living Will arises not from the need to deal with the issues of death and dying but from the need to preserve the patient's right of self-determination in health care beyond the time of incompetency. This right is not limited to patients with terminal diseases. The courts which have addressed this issue have confirmed that patients who are not terminally ill also have the right to continue to direct their own medical care, after the development of incompetency, through Living Wills. Because the concept is so basic to the formation of the comprehensive Living Will advocated in this book, cases upholding the right of non-terminal patients to control their own care will now be discussed in some detail.

The following cases involve patients with diseases not considered to be terminal who, while competent, asked that therapy be stopped and gained court approval to do so:

1. In *Grant*, a 25-year-old female with Batten's disease, who was said to be in an advanced stage of an incurable illness and suffering from severe and permanent mental and physical deterioration, was given the right to have life-sustaining treatment withheld.
2. In *McAfee*, a 42-year-old quadriplegic, victim of an auto accident, petitioned the court

---

* As we go to press, at least Arizona, Connecticut, New Jersey, Idaho, South Dakota, and West Virginia have added statutory provisions allowing declarants to direct discontinuation of care in the presence of permanent unconsciousness.

to order that his respirator be stopped and it was allowed.

3. In *In re Requena*, a 55-year-old with amyotrophic lateral sclerosis (Lou Gehrig's disease) refused a feeding tube when unable to swallow. This order was allowed by the court in spite of the fact that it would result in the patient's death.

4. In *Bartling*, a 70-year-old man with emphysema, chronic respiratory failure, atherosclerosis, abdominal aneurysm, and malignant tumor of the lung was allowed to order his respirator removed, the court saying:

If the right of the patient whose self-determination as to his own medical treatment is to have any meaning at all, it must be paramount to the interests of the hospital and the doctors. The right of a competent adult patient to refuse medical treatment is a constitutionally guaranteed right which must not be abridged.

5. In *Bouvia*, a 28-year-old cerebral palsy victim with a nasogastric tube sought removal of the tube. It caused her pain and had been inserted against her will. The court allowed its removal saying it would be "incongruous, if not monstrous [for physicians to force a woman suffering from cerebral palsy and quadriplegia] to live imprisoned . . . physically helpless [and] subject to ignominy, embarrassment, humiliation and dehumanizing aspects created by her helplessness."

6. In *Rodas*, a non-terminally ill father of young children, who was paralyzed from the neck down, unable to speak, and in pain, was permitted to refuse nutrition and hydration.

7. In *Satz*, the Florida Supreme Court held that a competent adult suffering from amyotrophic lateral sclerosis, who had no dependent children, had the right to direct his physicians to discontinue a respirator if the family was in agreement. [This particular case did not say what would happen if the family did not agree.]

8. In *Foster* v *Tourtellott*, the court held that a competent 67-year-old man with amyotrophic lateral sclerosis could order withdrawal of his respirator in spite of the opposition of his wife and children.

9. In *In the Matter of Golda Yoder*, a 76-year-old mother of seven with cirrhosis and persistent and painful post-operative infection died before a court opinion could be reached, but the court stated it would have supported her right to discontinue her care against the desires of her children if it had had a chance to decide.

10. In *In re Blodgett*, a 19-year-old competent man, paralyzed from the jaw down as the result of a driving accident, was allowed to order his respirator removed.

11. In *In re Culham*, a 57-year-old competent patient, suffering from amyotrophic lateral sclerosis, was allowed to order his respirator removed.

Besides the cases discussed in Principle 4 in which directives were found to be contrary to state interests, the author is unaware of other cases in which the request of a competent patient to discontinue care was refused.

The cases just enumerated refer to patients who were still competent at the time they requested therapy be stopped. The same results were reached in the following cases, in which surrogate decision makers requested discontinuation of therapy for incompetent patients who had clearly expressed their desires prior to becoming incompetent:

1. In *In re Lydia E. Hall Hospital*, the court ordered the discontinuance of renal dialysis in a 41-year-old comatose male in chronic renal failure who also had diabetes and brain damage and who had expressed the desire in writing that dialysis be stopped if he became comatose.

2. In *Leach*, a guardian was allowed to have the respirator stopped for an incompetent 72-year-old female with amyotrophic lateral sclerosis who, while competent, had clearly stated she did not want to be kept alive once the disease progressed to her present state.

3. In *Farrell*, the husband of a 37-year-old woman with amyotrophic lateral sclerosis was allowed to order the respirator stopped based on her prior expression of a desire to have it removed.

A slightly different situation arose in *A.B.* v *C.* In this case the patient became quadriplegic after an accident that resulted in a neck fracture. At the time of the accident, the patient wrote a Living Will in case of future incompetence. Although she did not want to stop the respirator immediately, she wanted to appoint another person to make that decision if she became incompetent. The New York court ruled that this could be done in spite of the fact that New York does not have a Living Will statute.

The following cases are also important because they are cases in which the request by a surrogate to stop treatment was denied, but the court indicated that had there been "clear and convincing" evidence of the patient's desires, such as a Living Will, the court would have followed its directives.

1. In *O'Conner*, a New York court required placement of a nasogastric tube to feed an elderly, severely mentally incapacitated patient for lack of "clear and convincing" evidence that the patient had made a firm and clear commitment while competent to decline such medical assistance.
2. In *In re Visbeck*, a New Jersey court required the placement of a gastrotomy feeding tube in a 90-year-old with minimum quality of life in the absence of any direction to the contrary from the patient.
3. In *Conroy*, a guardian sought the right to remove the nasogastric tube from an 84-year-old female who had organic brain syndrome which had caused the patient to become demented with very limited intellectual capacity. Her condition was irreversible. The New Jersey court refused to withdraw therapy because there was insufficient evidence of the patient's desires, but in so doing recognized that a Living Will would have constituted sufficient evidence of the patient's intent.
4. More recently, in *In re Guardianship of Browning*, the Second District Court of Appeals of Florida refused to permit the withdrawal of a nasogastric feeding tube from an 89-year-old woman who was severely brain damaged but in neither a terminal condition nor a persistent vegetative state. The woman had written a Living Will with the statutory directive regarding terminal illness and even included a statement requesting the withdrawal of nutrition if she became terminally ill. But she had *not* addressed a specific situation in which her medical condition fit exactly in to the narrow statutory definition of a terminal condition. Under these circumstances, the court found there was insufficient evidence of her desire to allow the court to condone the removal of the feeding tube.*

As these cases demonstrate, a properly worded Living Will leaving specific directives for diseases that are not terminal would probably be honored either directly by physicians or secondarily by the courts in spite of the fact such Living Wills are presently unusual.

PRINCIPLE 10: PHYSICIANS NEED NOT PERSONALLY COMPLY WITH A PATIENT'S DIRECTIVES

Physicians may not undermine a patient's directives, but they are not required to honor directives in a Living Will if they have personal conflicts in doing so. In this situation, the physician must transfer the patient's care to another physician who will follow the directives. This right of the physician to refuse to carry out personally a patient's directives to stop care was specifically accepted by a California court in *Conservatorship of Morrison* and supported by the Illinois court in the *Longeway* decision.

In some circumstances, however, this right of the physician is not honored. If, for example, the physician knows that a Living Will exists and fails to tell the patient he or she will not follow the directives so another physician can be found before a crisis, the physician may be forced to follow the directives. In Alaska, a physician who does not follow the Living Will directives may be prevented from charging for his or her services in the interim period until another physician is found to assume care.

* The Florida Supreme Court subsequently reversed the appeal court and allowed discontinuation of the feeding tube.

PRINCIPLE 11: AN INSTITUTION MAY OR MAY NOT BE REQUIRED TO HONOR A PATIENT'S REQUEST THAT LIFE-SUPPORT SYSTEMS BE DISCONTINUED

Health-care facilities that are unwilling to honor a patient's directives to withhold or withdraw medical care are usually permitted to transfer the patient to another facility. This option is especially available if the institution has written guidelines precluding compliance with such directives.

As decided in *Brophy*, the hospital did not have to stop tube feeding. The *Brophy* decision reads: "A patient's right to refuse medical treatment does not warrant such unnecessary intrusion upon the hospital's ethical integrity in the case." Subsequently the patient's guardian was authorized to remove her from the hospital to the care of another physician who would honor the patient's wishes.

If a health-care facility does not have written guidelines, or if the transfer of the patient is difficult or not in the patient's best interest, institutions are frequently forced by courts to follow the patient's directives against the institution's desires. This situation most likely would occur if a patient specifically requests to be treated in a particular facility.

Such a situation occurred in *Requena*, in which a 55-year-old with Lou Gehrig's disease was allowed to refuse a feeding tube when unable to swallow. The New Jersey court refused to issue an order to remove the patient to another institution as requested by the hospital in spite of the institutional policy against participating in the withholding of food and fluids.

Similarly, in *Rodas* a Colorado court required a nursing home to care for a man who was paralyzed from the neck down, unable to speak, and in constant pain who refused to permit further nutrition and hydration.

PRINCIPLE 12: HEALTH-CARE GIVERS SHOULD NOT BE THREATENED BY THE FEAR OF LEGAL ACTION FOR HONORING LIVING WILL DIRECTIVES

There has never been a case in which a health-care provider has been successfully sued for malpractice or found to have committed unprofessional conduct for following the directives of a Living Will document in good faith.

Even if judges were to question what a physician has done, they recognize the desirability of honoring Living Will directives without judicial involvement and are sympathetic to the pressures on physicians in the clinical setting. They have therefore been justifiably reluctant to rule against a physician who has honored a directive in good faith and are likely to continue to support the physician in the future.

PRINCIPLE 13: A COURT APPOINTED GUARDIAN OR CONSERVATOR MAY OR MAY NOT BE REQUIRED IN THE PRESENCE OF AN APPROPRIATE LIVING WILL

Most courts recognize that they are not the best decision makers and have tended to find that if there is "clear and convincing" evidence of a patient's desires or if there is a unanimity of opinion as to what should be done among the interested parties, health-care workers need not obtain court approval before following the patient's wishes. As a result, with the passage of time, it becomes easier to have directives of an appropriate Living Will followed without ever involving a court.

The evolving consensus rule appears to be that where there is clear evidence of the patient's desires and these desires are not contrary to accepted medical standards of care (i.e., would not constitute euthanasia), the directives can be followed in good faith without court approval or appointment of a guardian or conservator. Even in the absence of clear evidence of the patient's desires, if there is some evidence and there is agreement of the physicians, the family, and any guardian or conservator, the directives can be followed in good faith. If there is still doubt, concurrence of a patient advocate or an ombudsman or a bioethics committee may be sought. If such agreement is sought and there is still agreement, court approval is not necessary to remove life-support systems from a patient with a terminal disease or who is in a persistent vegetative state. If there is a disagreement, however, courts should be able to resolve it.

Unfortunately, while these are the evolving

standards, there is still enough variation among the jurisdictions that physicians may be left without sufficient guidance to proceed without judicial approval. The clearer the evidence, the greater the unanimity of the family, and the more in keeping any act is with standard medical care, the more likely the physician is to act on his or her own.

PRINCIPLE 14: THERE IS NO SET RULE AS TO WHO IS THE APPROPRIATE DECISION MAKER FOR AN INCOMPETENT PATIENT

Some, but not all states, have within their statutes a priority order of decision makers for patients who are no longer competent. Highest priority is given to a spouse, a guardian, a proxy appointed by the patient, or a combination thereof. In those states with such lists there is no conformity.

It is not even clear as yet how much authority a designated health-care proxy in a Living Will actually commands, but as with the Living Will itself, designation of a proxy clearly carries the strength of the patient's desires related to continued self-determination in health care and should be given top priority.

In Connecticut, even under the Living Will statute, the patient's directives in a Living Will must also be approved by the next of kin. This mandate is against all prevailing opinion which holds that the patient has the right to make the final decision. As stated by a New York court in *Collins* v *Davis*: "The family should not be able to overrule the competently expressed wishes of an elderly, incurably ill patient."*

PRINCIPLE 15: SOME STATES REQUIRE "CLEAR AND CONVINCING" EVIDENCE OF A PATIENT'S DESIRES. OTHERS DO NOT. LIVING WILLS FULFILL THIS REQUIREMENT, BUT THERE IS GREAT DISAGREEMENT IN THE ABSENCE OF SUCH AN ADVANCED DIRECTIVE

Probably the most disputed "death with dignity" issue is the question of how decisions should be made for incompetent patients who have not left advance directives. The dispute centers around whether the substitute decision maker should use what is called "substituted judgment" approach or the "best interest" approach.

Most states have adopted use of the substituted judgment approach. This approach requires the surrogate decision maker to decide in accordance with what the patient would have wanted if still able to decide. Many jurisdictions accept this substituted judgment approach. Nevertheless, there is still great variation in how much evidence regarding the patient's wishes is required before the substitute decision maker can decide to stop life-support systems.

Many courts say they require "clear and convincing" evidence, but even within this definition there is still great variation. For example, in *O'Conner*, the New York court said that to qualify as "clear and convincing" evidence, prior statements must evince "a firm and settled commitment" to the termination of life-sustaining technology "under the circumstances like those presented" and must be "more than immediate reactions to the unsettling experience of seeing or hearing of another's unnecessarily prolonged death." In this case, the court stated Living Wills would be given far greater weight than oral statements.

Other courts accept far more remote evidence. For instance, in *Romeo*, the court accepted, as "clear and convincing" evidence, conversations about the Karen Quinlan matter which had occurred eleven years earlier.

A minority of courts have accepted the best interest standard. According to the Washington court in *Grant*, this approach requires an evaluation of the patient's current condition, degree of pain, loss of dignity, prognosis, and the risks, side effects, and benefits of each treatment option. Other courts have also added the patient's quality of life and the patient's interest in preserving the family's interest, but still other courts find these additions objectionable.

Many courts seem to combine the two approaches, using substituted judgment when it is reasonably certain and best interest when the patient's desires are not known. This combination

---

* In June 1991, the Connecticut legislature replaced the previous Living Will statute giving the state a new law broadly supportive of the individual's right of self-determination in health care.

has been specifically sanctioned in Arizona and Washington.

The most complicated system has been developed in New Jersey, a leader in the field of "death with dignity" considerations. In the often quoted decision in *Conroy*, the New Jersey Supreme Court suggested a four tier approach:

1. If there is "clear and convincing" evidence of the patient's desires, it is to be followed.
2. If the patient is in a persistent vegetative state, therapy can be stopped if family and guardian conclude, after rendering their best judgment, that the patient, if competent, would desire termination.
3. If the above does not apply, the surrogate decision maker should use a "limited-objective" best interest standard, which means that there is "some trustworthy evidence that the patient would have refused the treatment" and the burdens of prolonging life "markedly outweigh" any physical, emotional, or intellectual benefits deriving from that life.
4. If there is no trustworthy evidence of the patient's desires, under a "pure objective standard," care can be terminated only when:
   a. the burdens of prolonged life "clearly and markedly" outweigh the benefits;
   b. treatment would cause such "recurring unavoidable and severe pain" that administering it would be "inhumane."

This issue of what is the accepted basis for making a substituted judgment was the key issue in the recent decision, *Cruzan* v *Director, Missouri Department of Health*, in which the U.S. Supreme Court reviewed the decision of the Missouri Supreme Court in *Cruzan* v *Harmon*, previously discussed. The holding in that case, which greatly increased interest in Living Wills, was that in the absence of a Living Will, Missouri had the right to refuse to allow the withholding of nutrition and hydration in the patient who had been in a persistent vegetative state for many years. The legal basis for this decision was that Missouri had the right to define strictly the need for "clear and convincing" evidence of the patient's desire before a surrogate decision could direct that therapy be discontinued. Under such strict definition, the need for "clear and convincing" evidence essentially requires a writing, such as a Living Will.

The importance of recognizing this conflict among the jurisdictions as to what constitutes enough evidence to discontinue therapy in the absence of an advanced directive is not in knowing the law but in realizing how much simpler it is when there is a Living Will. A Living Will constitutes the next best evidence of the patient's desires, after the patient's own present statement, and constitutes a method of avoiding these conflicts.

PRINCIPLE 16: THE PATIENT'S KNOWN DESIRES SHOULD ALWAYS BE CONTROLLING

The prevailing opinion among court decisions is that the known preference of the patient should control the decision reached by a surrogate decision maker, whoever that is. In fact, even when a court specifically allows other considerations, evidence of the patient's desires always seem to be controlling, as decided in *Golda Yoder* and *Foster* discussed earlier.

PRINCIPLE 17: A PATIENT IS PRESUMED TO BE COMPETENT UNTIL PROVEN OTHERWISE

Usually the determination of incompetency is made by a court decision after a hearing. This requirement, however, has not been followed with reference to Living Wills, in which the determination of incompetency is either left to the physician by statutory direction or by general acceptance under the common law.

An interesting case that discusses this issue is *In re Yetter*, a Pennsylvania decision in which the brother of a schizophrenic woman wanted a court to appoint him conservator of his sister to force her to undergo diagnostic tests for cancer. During her previous lucid times she had refused such tests and at the time of the hearing still did not want them, although she was no longer competent. The court denied the request that the woman be forced to undergo the tests.

A problem regarding incompetency arises

when a formerly competent patient has written a Living Will that directs care be withheld or withdrawn, but the same patient, now incompetent, directs otherwise. Legally, the previously written words of the competent person would take precedence over the spoken words of the now incompetent person, but, under the circumstances, physicians always choose to continue life-support systems.

This procedure is reasonable and consistent with the general principle that patients are presumed to be competent. It also goes along with the general principle recognizing the sanctity of life.

PRINCIPLE 18: SURROGATE DECISION-MAKING PROCESS SIMPLIFIED

Because so few people take the time to write Living Wills, alternative means of simplifying the surrogate decision-making process are now being advocated. These methods basically allow the declarant to name another person to speak in their stead if they become incapacitated instead of making specific directions. Such proxy designations have the advantage of being more responsive to situations as they develop, but they negate the personal directions permitted by the Living Will.

While many Living Will statutes now suggest including provisions for designation of decision-making proxies, the exact obligations and rights of such proxies when not clearly delineated in the document have not as yet been adequately determined under the common law to recommend routinely that they be included.

A case specifically recognizing the durable power of attorney for health-care decision is *Peter*, in which a close friend holding a health-care power of attorney was allowed to discontinue the nasogastric tube in a 65-year-old man who was in a persistent vegetative state.

Section Five

RELIGION AND LIVING WILLS

Religion's deep concern with the dying process and with conflicts between the rights of the individual versus the rights of society has led to frequent comments on "death with dignity" issues. Overwhelmingly, these comments have supported the rights of the individual as expressed in Living Wills.

The general approach of religion was nicely summarized in a resolution adopted by the General Assembly of the Unitarian Universalist Association in Palm Springs, California, in June, 1988 which reads as follows:

THE RIGHT TO DIE WITH DIGNITY

Guided by our belief as Unitarian Universalists that human life has inherent dignity, which may be compromised when life is extended beyond the will or ability of a person to sustain that dignity; and believing that it is every person's inviolable right to determine in advance the course of action to be taken in the event that there is no reasonable expectation of recovery from extreme physical or mental disability; and

WHEREAS, medical knowledge and technology make possible the mechanical prolongation of life; and

WHEREAS, such prolongation may cause unnecessary suffering and/or loss of dignity while providing little or nothing of benefit to the individual; and

WHEREAS, such procedures have an impact upon a health-care system in which services are limited and inequitably distributed; and

WHEREAS, differences exist among people over religious, moral, and legal implications of administering aid in dying when an individual of sound mind has voluntarily asked for such aid; and obstacles exist within our society against providing support for an individual's declared wish to die; and

WHEREAS, many counselors, clergy, and health-care personnel value prolongation of life regardless of the quality of life or will to live;

THEREFORE BE IT RESOLVED: that the Unitarian Universalist Association calls upon its congregations and individual Unitarian Universalists to examine attitudes and practices in our society relative to the ending of life, as well as those in other countries and cultures; and

BE IT FURTHER RESOLVED: that Unitarian Universalists reaffirm their support for the Living Will, as declared in a 1978 resolution of the General Assembly, declare support for the Durable Power of Attorney for Health Care, and seek assurance that both instruments will be honored; and

BE IT FURTHER RESOLVED: that Unitarian Universalists advocate the right to self-determination in dying, and the release from civil or criminal penalties of those who, under proper safeguards, act to honor the right of terminally ill patients to select the time of their own deaths; and

BE IT FURTHER RESOLVED: that Unitarian Universalists advocate safeguards against abuses by those who would hasten death contrary to an individual's desire; and

BE IT FINALLY RESOLVED: that the Unitarian Universalists, acting through their congregations, memorial societies, and appropriate organizations, inform and petition legislators to support legislation that will create legal protection for the right to die with dignity, in accordance with one's own choice.

The Vatican Document on Euthanasia reads in part:

When inevitable death is imminent in spite of the means used, it is permitted in conscience to take the decision to refuse forms of treatment that would only secure a precarious and burdensome prolongation of life, so long as the normal care due to the sick person in similar cases is not interrupted. In such circumstances the doctor has no reason to reproach himself with failing to help the person in danger, and

It is also permissible to make do with the normal means that medicine can offer. Therefore one can not impose on anyone the obligation to have recourse to a technique which is already in use but which carries a risk or is burdensome. Such a refusal is not the equivalent of suicide; on the contrary, it should be considered as an acceptance of the human condition, or a wish to avoid the application of a medical procedure disproportionate to the results that can be expected, or a desire not to impose excessive expense on the family or the community.

A combined statement by the United Methodist and Roman Catholic leaders reads:

When a person is dying and medical intervention can at best prolong a minimal level of life at great cost to human dignity, structures of care and use of medical technology should focus on maximizing the individual's capacity for awareness, feeling, and relationships with family and community. Decisions that subordinate the humane dying of a terminally ill man or woman to the technological imperative, or personal or institutional self-interest—legal, financial, professional—are not consistent with Christian values and traditions.

The right of persons to exercise autonomy and to be self-determining is protected in a just society by norms and procedures that involve the patient as an active participant in medical treatment decisions. The Christian community supports such personal rights because it views all persons as created in the image of God, endowed with freedom and called to accountability before God and their covenant community for decisions they make.

Other Protestant denominations have spoken in support of Living Wills in the following words:

The supreme value in our religious heritage is placed on the person in wholeness, the person in freedom, the person in integrity and dignity. When illness takes away those abilities we associate with full personhood, leaving one so impaired that what is most valuable and precious is gone,

we may well feel that the mere continuance of the body by machine or drugs is a violation of the person.

Nothing in Jewish or Christian tradition presumes that a physician has a mandate to impose his or her wishes and skills upon patients for the sake of prolonging the length of their dying where those patients are diagnosed as terminally ill and do not wish the interventions of the physician. People who are dying have as much freedom as other living persons to accept or to refuse medical treatment where that treatment provides no cure for their ailment. Thus the freedom of the patient to choose his or her own style for the remainder of his or her life and the method and time for dying is enhanced.

We believe it is ethically and theologically proper for a person to wish to avoid artificial and/or painful prolongation of a terminal illness and for him or her to execute a Living Will or similar document of instructions.

—Action of The Council for Christian Social Action of the United Church of Christ, February 17, 1973

The Presbyterian Church calls upon its members to:

a. Select their physicians with regard not only to the skillfulness of the medical care that they can provide but also for their values regarding human life and community, whenever such a choice is available.

b. Take time to reflect on their own values and discuss these with family members, close friends, and their clergy.

c. Speak with their physicians about their concerns regarding care and become educated about their conditions in order to permit informed decision-making.

d. Provide instructions (and designate two agents to carry out instructions) with regard to extraordinary therapies and treatments to prolong life.

—From the proceedings of the 195th General Assembly (1983) of the Presbyterian Church.

On May 15, 1989 the American Jewish Congress issued a policy statement concerning decisions to forgo life-sustaining treatment. Some of the highlights follow:

First, it is the AJ Congress' view that public policy must continue to support the right of decision-capable patients to decide about their own health care. This includes the right to choose maximum appropriate medical treatment and a broad, though not absolute, right to refuse life-sustaining treatment, e.g., cardiopulmonary resuscitation, mechanical ventilation, and artificial nutrition and hydration.

The desire of individuals for greater control over life-sustaining treatment decisions is legitimate: the existence of a treatment should not itself create an obligation to employ it in every instance. Rather, medical treatments must be employed to serve human ends; that is, they must be used to promote the objectives of the patient.

While most members of our society, including Jews, will feel a desire and obligation to accept treatment that may prolong life, such decisions must remain a matter of personal conscience. In this most sensitive area, it is imperative that public policy respect the pluralistic nature of society and the diversity of views even within communities.

Second, the AJ Congress supports public policies to enable individuals to create advance directives, such as Living Wills and health-care proxies. Typically, patients lack decision-making capacity at the time life-sustaining treatment decisions must be made. Thus, our commitment to patient self-determination necessitates recognition of advance directives. Without such devices, patients have little assurance that their wishes about life-sustaining treatment will be honored.

Accordingly, the AJ Congress favors legislation authorizing advance directives in those jurisdictions where legislation is necessary to recognize validity. However, each proposal must be considered on its own merits. Particular care should be taken to ensure that a proposal does indeed promote and preserve patient self-determination; some current Living Will laws appear to limit patients' ability to refuse treatment by imposing excessive substantive restrictions or procedural requirements.

The AJ Congress finds particular merit in policies that legitimize and encourage the use of durable powers of attorney for health care, or "health-care proxies." An adult uses this device to appoint another to make health-care decisions for himself or herself in the event that he or she loses the capacity to make those decisions personally.

The health-care proxy is advantageous for a variety of reasons, among them that it identifies an individual who can convey and interpret the patient's wishes, or assess the patient's interests, with respect to the unanticipated decisions that must be confronted. Moreover, the proxy approach more closely approximates the ideal of informed consent because the agent can receive current information about the patient's condition and discuss the patient's case with all involved before arriving at a decision. Significantly, the designation of an agent is a procedural device only; an adult can appoint an agent to ensure that life-sustaining treatment is provided, if that is his or her wish.

While the above typifies the approach taken by most leaders of Conservative and Reform congregations, leaders of the Orthodox Jewish church tend to be antagonistic to forgoing life-support systems, especially when doing so involves the withdrawing of previously initiated care.

For additional information regarding the Orthodox Jewish approach to Living Wills, the reader can write to the following address:

Halachic Living Will
Aqudath Israel of America
84 William Street
New York, NY 10038

Section Six

INTRODUCTION TO THE COMPREHENSIVE LIVING WILL

The Comprehensive Living Will Form included in this book (hereinafter referred to as the "Form") addresses those clinical situations in which a Living Will document is likely to be important. It includes alternative provisions which allow you to initial your preferences. Except for the statutory form documents in Article Eleventh, any other articles may be modified by simply adding phrases in the margins or crossing out existing provisions, which should then be initialed. In Article Tenth, you may add specific directives covering areas inadequately covered in the Form to meet your specific needs. After completing Article Tenth, if the document inadequately represents your desires, seek assistance from a local attorney knowledgeable in the field.

First consider the six basic decisions you must make to complete the Form. The information following the questions is intended to help you reach these decisions.

The Basic Questions

1. If you become unable to make or communicate health-care decisions *and you will never get better*, do you want to be allowed to die in peace by forsaking life-prolonging care in the following situations:
   A. In the presence of a terminal disease?
   B. If you were to become permanently unconscious?
   C. If you suffered from severe and irreversible mental deterioration?
   D. If an existing disease progresses to the point where you are incompetent?
   E. If a stroke causes permanent paralysis and loss of the ability to communicate with the world?
2. If you elect to forsake medical care in any of the above situations, do you only want to forsake mechanical treatments? Or, do you also want your physicians to stop non-pain medications, surgery, diagnostic testing, artificially administered food and nutrition, and cardio-pulmonary resuscitation (CPR)? (CPR refers to those techniques used to resuscitate people whose hearts or lungs have stopped functioning.)
3. If you are permanently unconscious and elect to forgo medical care, do you want to rely on your physicians to decide when it is appropriate to stop treatment or do you want them to wait a specified length of time before making such a decision?
4. If you are a woman of childbearing age, do you want medical care to stop even if you are pregnant?
5. Do you want to name a health-care proxy to help insure that your directives are followed and to make additional decisions if required?
6. If you do want a health-care proxy, whom do you want to make decisions for you and what duties do you expect him or her to undertake?

When filling out the Form, in addition to provisions which incorporate your decisions to the above questions, there are many which do not require your input. These provisions are intended to avoid specific legal problems which can interfere with the honoring of your directives. Please do not be turned off by the repetition of many of these provisions and the resulting length of the Form.

INSTRUCTIONS/EXPLANATIONS FOR THE COMPREHENSIVE LIVING WILL FORM

Instructions are printed in boldface type. Information regarding the various provisions are printed in normal type. (NOTE: When a provision in the Form is self-explanatory or repetitive, it may not be referred to in this section.)

NOTICE TO DECLARANT

The Form begins with a Notice Statement. This statement assures others that you, the declarant, were aware of the information the Form contains at the time you signed it. The statement is also required in some states as part of the designation of a proxy decision maker.

Paragraph (1) points out that you have executed the Living Will Declaration for both social and legal purposes. It indicates that the naming of a proxy is optional, as is the naming of a specific health-care facility in which you would like to be treated; see Article Tenth.)

Paragraph (2) directs a designated health-care proxy to first consider your desires when making decisions. It also points out that if you do not name a proxy, you still expect health-care providers to honor your directives as written.

You should discuss the Living Will declarations with your designated proxy and your physician to determine if they will resist honoring your directives. If a conflict exists and is not resolved, an alternative proxy and/or physician should be considered.

Paragraph (3) points out the concern of many physicians that the patient may change his or her outlook after writing a directive. Therefore, it is wise to indicate periodically your continued agreement with the previous directives by re-signing the document. (NOTE: California requires such re-affirmation every five years.)

This paragraph also suggests the best way of revoking a Living Will is to deface the original document by crossing out the front and signature pages in ink, writing thereon "I revoke," and signing.

There is little reason to deny a proxy the power to review and disclose health-care information as discussed in paragraph (4), but you can do so by inserting a provision in Article Ninth in which you designate your health-care proxy(ies).

Paragraph (5) points out that even though you used a form declaration, you were aware of the possibility of making deletions or additions if you so desired.

INTRODUCTORY PARAGRAPH

The introductory paragraph simply identifies you as the declarant and makes the statement that this document supersedes previous health-care directives in the form of a Living Will.

ARTICLE FIRST: PERSONAL STATEMENT REGARDING THE COMPREHENSIVE LIVING WILL

Article First explains the working of the Form and recruits support for your directives. No decisions have to be made here, but if there are any statements you wish to change, do so by writing in the margins or by crossing out and initialing unwanted phrases.

ARTICLE SECOND: STATUTORY TERMINAL CONDITION

Provision II(A)(1) gives you the choice offered by the state's statutory Living Will Declaration to forsake life-support systems if you are suffering from an irreversible terminal condition.

Provision II(A)(2) gives you the opportunity to request continuation of life-support systems. It indicates to others that you had the opportunity to continue therapy as well as to refuse therapy.

Unless you want therapy continued, initial in the parenthesis after "II(A)(1)," sign on the signature line, and print your name on the next line as indicated. Cross out provision "II(A)(2)" using a few lines.

Provisions II(B) through II(D) attempt to overcome obstacles to qualifying under the state statute, such as failing to sign the appropriate form in Article Eleventh.

ARTICLE THIRD: NON-STATUTORY TERMINAL CONDITION

Article Third is intended to expand your Living Will declaration for use in states which do not have Living Will statutes. It is to cover the situation in which your condition is considered terminal but is precluded from so qualifying by a state's narrow definition of "terminal disease" or "terminal condition."

It employs a very broad definition of terminal condition which requires only that it would eventually lead to death without treatment and that even with treatment there is no reasonable chance of ever returning to competency. The phrase in Section III(B)(2)(b) is added to avoid potential uncertainty which could occur if the temporary elimination of pain medications would result in a temporary return to consciousness but only with return of unacceptable pain.

This article is not appropriate if you suffer from a dementia. (See Article Sixth.)

Unless you wish to restrict coverage of the Living Will to the narrowly defined limits of a Living Will statute, Provision III(A)(1) should be initialed, signed, and your name inserted as above and Provision III(A)(2) crossed out.

Provision III(C) is intended to call attention to the fact that this article was executed by the declarant with the intent of covering two distinct situations as discussed.

ARTICLE FOURTH: PERMANENT UNCONSCIOUSNESS

Article Fourth includes directives to be followed if you were to become permanently unconscious.

Unless you would want to be kept alive in a state of permanent unconsciousness, initial after IV(A)(1), fill in your name and signature as before, and cross out IV(A)(2).

Provision IV(B) addresses an important consideration in dealing with the form of unconsciousness referred to as the persistent vegetative state (PVS).

Patients in a PVS can often be maintained for years by providing nutrition by artificial means, hydration, and occasional antibiotics. These patients may show cyclic wakening and sleep patterns and respond reflexively to stimuli, but they never express any evidence of integrated brain function or the ability to respond coherently to external events.

PVS, however, is not necessarily irreversible. Therefore, it is inappropriate to stop supportive therapy immediately upon making the diagnosis. Other factors must be considered. The longer the patient is unresponsive and the older the patient, the less chance there is for recovery. In addition, the likelihood of recovery is influenced by the cause of the PVS, recovery being most likely when the PVS results from a head injury.

You have two reasonable approaches when dealing with this uncertainty. You may either rely on your physicians to decide when enough time has passed or you may specify a length of time which physicians must wait before determining if the chance of recovery is so slight as to justify discontinuation of life-support systems.

For those who would consider adding a time requirement to the physicians' judgment, the following statement is taken from the report of the Council on Scientific Affairs and the Council on Ethical and Judicial Affairs of the American Medical Association discussing PVS as presented in June of 1989:

> To be more specific about guidelines, with the exception of children, in whom too little evidence exists to offer reliable conclusions, few if any patients who remain vegetative following cardiac arrest or similar asphyxial injuries [poor oxygen supply to the brain due to problems in the lungs] recover after one month and essentially none will regain cognition [the ability to perceive, think, remember] after three vegetative months. Patients with less severe, purely anoxic [lack of oxygen] injuries (e.g., from carbon monoxide poisoning) do somewhat better, but even in such cases recovery of consciousness after three months is limited to rare patients considerably younger than 40 years. The prognosis for cognitive return in patients younger than 40 years with head injury or subarachnoid hemorrhage [bleeding within the skull] is somewhat better than the

above, but still relatively poor. Accurate percentages are lacking, but nevertheless, sufficient numbers of patients in these categories begin to show at least a measure of cognition between three and six months that decisions about continuing care should be deferred beyond that time. A few reports describe a return of cognition even beyond the six-month time in persons younger than 25 years. Some of these may have represented patients who entered an unrecognized "locked-in" state shortly after reawakening from a coma-causing injury.* Ultimately, all have been severely disabled.

These rare examples notwithstanding, data indicate with high probability the lengths of time, according to age and the nature of disease, when patients can safely be regarded as having reached a permanent, hopeless vegetative state. Even in young persons who have experienced head trauma, a conservative criterion for the diagnosis of PVS would be observed unawareness for at least 12 months. Cognitive recovery after six months is vanishingly rare in patients older than 50 years. If the handful of reported occurrences of cognitive recovery in patients with PVS are divided by the total estimated number of PVS cases in this country, the odds of recovery are less than one in 1,000.** The risk of prognostic error from widespread use of the above criterion is so small that a decision that incorporates it as a prognostic conclusion seems fully justified.

The Form allows you to either rely totally on the medical opinion of the physicians by crossing out IV(B)(2) or to add a time requirement by initialing IV(B)(2).

In deciding on the length of time to delay it should be appreciated that delay is not associated with suffering. The main aim of a Living Will Declaration covering PVS is to prevent a situation in which your body would be kept alive but unresponsive for years without any hope of regaining significant function. Because there is no pain or suffering requiring rapid relief, waiting a period of time is reasonable.

Based on the AMA report, many declarants between 25 and 50 years of age would choose to require 12 months of time to pass before a decision is made, while declarants over 50 are likely to choose to require six months, but these numbers, which are included on the Form, are arbitrary and can not be specifically recommended. Each declarant has to make that decision for him-

self or herself. Whatever time requirement is specified, before a life-support system is stopped there must also be agreement among the physicians that there is no reasonable chance of recovery. This issue would be an appropriate one to discuss with your physician.

Initial after IV(B)(2) if you wish to add a time requirement. You may strike out the included time periods and substitute different time periods if you so desire. If you do, initial next to the inserted numbers where they appear on the form. If you wish to rely on the judgment of the physician, cross out the entire paragraph.

Provision IV(C) is similar to provision III(C) above.

ARTICLE FIFTH: ADDITIONAL DIRECTIVES / ARTICLES SECOND THROUGH FOURTH

Provision V(A) represents a major addition to most Living Will forms. It works in conjunction with directives in Articles Second through Fourth for situations in which you are no longer competent and are suffering from an irreversible condition which will result in death without ever allowing even a brief return to a meaningful life. Under these conditions most declarants consider the use of medications or surgery or the methods of cardio-pulmonary resuscitation (such as the use of an electrical shock to control the heart's rhythm) no different than the use of a respirator or a heart pump.

The same reasoning now leads most Living Will declarants to direct that nutrition and hydration be discontinued if there is no chance for a return to a meaningful life.

Unless you specifically want certain forms of treatment continued, initial within each of the five parentheses provided under Provision V(A).

Provision V(B) relates to the undecided issue as to whether or not states have the right to preclude the honoring of Living Will directives in a woman who is pregnant. As this situation has not been addressed specifically in the courts, the author can not assure the reader that this directive would be honored even if initialed.

---

* EDITOR'S NOTE: A neurologist should be able to tell the difference.
** EDITOR'S NOTE: This estimated chance of recovery is much better than the three per 100,000 noted in the recent *Cruzan* decision.

If you desire to request that therapy be stopped even if you are pregnant, initial in the parenthesis after V(B), sign, and write in your name as directed.

This provision does not direct stopping therapy if an unborn child is likely to be a healthy newborn because it is unlikely a physician or court would permit honoring such a directive.

Provision V(C) is included as a reminder that the so-called comfort care provision of many statutes should be limited to those treatments that are required for the relief of discomfort in the patient as they then exist, not as it would have been perceived at the time the Living Will was written.

ARTICLE SIXTH: END-STAGE DEMENTIA

The form declaration in Article Sixth is totally different from any statutory Living Will form. Under common law theory, however, a directive to forgo specific medical therapy if you were to develop a progressive dementia due to Alzheimer's disease or multiple strokes should be honored just as it would be for a terminal disease or PVS.

It is to be hoped that any remaining uncertainty will be removed by court decisions in the near future. If this right is confirmed in a few cases, it will validate all previously written Living Wills with provisions covering end-stage dementia and establish that court intervention is not required before such a directive is honored.

The fear of becoming a burden to others or losing one's dignity as the result of an end-stage dementia is a major reason people choose to execute Living Wills. Unfortunately, with no directive, care will always be continued. If this is against your desires, you should specifically include this article. Such a Living Will directive has a high chance of being honored if it is specific enough in describing the situation in which you want therapy withheld.

If the declarant specifically wants to include end-stage dementia as a reason to limit medical care, initial after VI(A)(1), sign, and fill in your name as before, and cross out VI(A)(2). If you do not want to limit care in end-stage dementia, initial and sign in VI(A)(2).

It is difficult to define end-stage dementia in a way that would be acceptable to all readers. The definition used in the Form is an attempt to define it in objective terms, meaning that others can tell whether the definition applies.

Many declarants who choose to include this article may prefer to write in their own definition for end-stage dementia. If you do, try to describe a situation in such a way that others, most important, your proxy, can determine with as much certainty as possible.

Remember, courts may rightfully question borderline situations but will have little reason not to honor directives in advanced cases when a person is essentially unresponsive due to brain destruction.

Change the definition of end-stage dementia if you feel there is another which more accurately reflects your particular views. Or, you may sign the directive and then add additional thoughts in Article Tenth.

Some declarants are particularly worried by the possibility of being kept alive for years after suffering a disabling stroke. In drafting a provision to address this concern, the following must be considered:

(1) Some patients who suffer a stroke become permanently unconscious, and would be covered by Article Fourth.

(2) Some patients suffer multiple strokes and develop a dementia almost identical to that in Alzheimer's disease. They would be covered by the provisions in VI(A) and VI(B).

(3) Most patients who survive strokes recover mental capacity and are capable of executing a directive covering a chronic irreversible condition under the following Article Seventh if they wish.

(4) Patients who suffer from strokes usually improve over a period of a few months after the initial insult. There should therefore be a time delay after the insult before decisions are made similar to the delay with PVS, but not necessarily as long.

(5) A Living Will directive is therefore only needed to address the remaining situation in which, after full recovery is achieved, the declarant is not permanently unconscious, does not experience the full cognitive loss of a dementia, but is incompetent or of questionable competency to make decisions. Even in this situation, a directive to forsake care should not take effect if the patient expresses a desire for continued care.

(6) Even with these limitations, it is common to find a family with no guidance in how to decide for a loved one who is bed-ridden, substantially paralyzed, unable to enjoy life, not outwardly desirous of living, but not competent enough to clearly direct discontinuation of care.

Provision VI(C) is a suggested provision which a declarant might want to include to deal with this potential situation.

Provision VI(D) is a repeat of Provision V(A) but is included to allow the declarant the opportunity to make different choices than he or she would make when dealing with terminal diseases. For instance, the declarant may want to be given antibiotics if he or she suffers from dementia but not if he or she has a terminal disease.

Carefully initial the forms of therapy which you would *not* want if you were suffering from an end-stage dementia.

Provision VI(E) specifically directs the person to be consulted by the attending physician regarding the discontinuation therapy in case of an end-stage dementia. If several are asked for approval, someone, for personal reasons, might not accept discontinuation of therapy. This provision limits this process to the single individual designated in Article Ninth and is a major reason for selecting a proxy.

ARTICLE SEVENTH: CHRONIC, PROGRESSIVE, IRREVERSIBLE CONDITION

Article Seventh should only be employed if you have a particular medical condition and are concerned about future care.

There are several cases where courts have directed health-care providers to honor directives which limit the use of life-support systems in patients with chronic illnesses. Directives under this article can not be guaranteed to be legally binding because they fall outside Living Will statutes. Nevertheless, patients with these diseases would probably be granted their right of self-determination through directives in Living Wills.

The paragraph in VII(A) provides background, the nature of the diagnosed condition, and the reasons for writing advance directives, while VII(B) provides a formal directive.

If you have been diagnosed with such a disease and wish to leave specific directives as to your future medical care, fill in the required information in VII(A) and add your name and signature in VII(B).

As in Article Sixth, the provisions of VII(C) should be individually addressed after carefully considering the nature of the underlying disease. If this section is applicable, you might state specific instructions in Article Tenth after consulting with your physician to find out what conditions are likely to arise.

Carefully initial those forms of therapy which you do *not* want as part of treatment of your present condition if it progressed to the point where you were incompetent and there was no reasonable hope that competency would ever be restored.

Paragraph VII(D) is similar to VI(E) and is used for the same reason.

ARTICLE EIGHTH: MISCELLANEOUS PROVISIONS

Provision VIII(A) is a so-called severability clause which insures that if any one or more provisions in the document are found not to be legal in any jurisdiction, it will not influence the legality of all other provisions.

Provision VIII(B) is required because of the use of different terminology in different states and the desire to keep the comprehensive Living Will valid in all states.

Provision VIII(C) gives the Living Will and your designated health-care proxy priority over previous health-care directives which might have been given in a durable power of attorney. Be careful not to void nonhealth-care decisions under such previous durable powers of attorney.

Provision VIII(D) is required because this document has been improperly labeled a "will." Care must therefore be taken to avoid it being inadvertently revoked by the wording of a subsequent regular will which typically begins, "I hereby revoke any previous will made by me."

Provision VIII(E) corresponds to statements in most state statutes which (1) preclude euthanasia, (2) require treatment for pain or discomfort, yet

(3) recognize that pain medication may hasten death.

Provision VIII(F) places within the Living Will document a provision extending immunity to those who honor the directives in a Living Will Declaration. It is highly advisable because such immunity is poorly provided under the common law.

Provision VIII(G) attempts to correct any procedural problems which may have been inadvertently introduced in the document. It is most important with regard to signing formalities.

Provision VIII(H) is desirable because states may require that Living Wills be re-executed after a certain number of years. This provision would provide that the Living Will be honored as presented under common law even if it was not honored under a statute because of such time limitation.

Provision VIII(I) explains the signed reaffirmation suggested by the author.

Provision VIII(J) attempts to deal with the difficult situation which occasionally arises when medical personnel other than the usual attending physicians are called to care for a patient in an emergency. It is unlikely that this paragraph will be held legally binding, but its inclusion should at least make those caring for you aware of the problems which are likely to occur when emergency care is requested for a person who no longer wants to be treated aggressively.

Provision VIII(L) is an attempt to deal reasonably with a situation in which a physician or health-care facility might find it objectionable to honor a Living Will directive.

If you do not want to include any of these provisions, you may cross them out, but it is not necessary to do so.

ARTICLE NINTH: HEALTH-CARE PROXY DESIGNATION

The duties and powers of a health-care proxy named in your Living Will may be influenced by both the statutory and common law of the state in which you receive care. Nevertheless, naming a health-care proxy with specific powers as is done in the Form is almost certain to produce substantial authority in all states.

If you intend to include Articles Sixth (end-stage dementia) and/or Seventh (chronic, progressive, irreversible condition), the need for a designated proxy is even greater than it is with Articles Second through Fourth. The need is greater for these directives because they are further from established law and physicians will welcome someone with whom to confer before making their final decision.

It is important that the proxy know your desires and share your general beliefs about health care at the end of life. If you know of no one who can serve this function, you may wish to rely on health-care personnel.

Most states favor relatives as designated proxies, but only Florida requires that an attorney-in-fact for health care be a relative. Many commentators feel that a close friend of long acquaintance is equally appropriate. The use of a treating physician as a designated proxy is usually not allowed.

If you choose not to name a proxy, and your physician is unable to make decisions based on the information in the Living Will, a court will appoint an impartial person as a guardian of your person (different names are used in different states) to make decisions on your behalf. Designation of a proxy is usually preferred, but there are people who do not have appropriate family or friends, or prefer not to burden them with life-and-death decisions.

If you wish to designate a health-care proxy, fill in the blanks in the first paragraph as indicated.

The Form lists a number of duties which can be delegated to a health-care proxy under various state statutes. The wording of the proxy designation in the Form would probably cover all legally accepted duties in most states. It is advisable to give specific directives (as suggested) to verify the range of decisions you want to delegate to your proxy. Doing so may also allow your proxy to perform such duties even if they do not fall within the powers granted by the statute of the state.

If you want to exclude any of the six suggested powers, cross out the provision and initial.

It is recommended that you designate more than one health-care proxy, but, if after filling out the comprehensive Living Will form you feel there is only one person you want to act on your behalf, it is better to cross out the place for alternatives than to designate additional alternate proxies.

Fill in the appropriate information for successor proxies for health care or cross out the sections for such appointments.

Many states have recently passed laws which specifically authorize a special kind of proxy designation called a Power of Attorney for Health Care. These statutes authorize the naming of a proxy to make health-care decisions independent of a Living Will, but the exact nature of the decisions the proxy can make for the declarant varies greatly from state to state. Although many lawyers presently advocate signing two separate documents, a Living Will and a Power of Attorney for Health Care, most commentators believe that a combination of the two in a single document like the Form is a preferable approach. If you live in one of the states which authorizes such a Power of Attorney for Health Care you may want to sign such a document being careful to name the same proxy as you do in the Living Will. (At present, form documents for California, Connecticut, District of Columbia, Georgia, Illinois, Kansas, Kentucky, Massachusetts, Mississippi, Nevada, New York, Ohio, Oregon, Pennsylvania, Rhode Island, Tennessee, Texas, Vermont, Wisconsin, and Wyoming can be obtained by sending two dollars to Hastings House Book Publishers, 141 Halstead Avenue, Mamaroneck, NY 10543. Be sure to specify the state form you desire.) We do not routinely recommend such a document because of the great variability of powers granted to proxies in the various states and the possibility that such a document may actually limit, not expand, your right of self-determination in health care.

ARTICLE TENTH: GUIDANCE PROVISIONS

These provisions, modeled after the Minnesota Living Will statute, allow you to put into words additional thoughts not covered in the form part of the document. If you feel your desires have been covered in the Form, do not comment.

Your comments may take the form of new directives or may clarify your wishes regarding previous directives. If you are concerned about the validity of such directives, consult an attorney who knows the common law of your state.

ARTICLE ELEVENTH: STATE LIVING WILL FORM DECLARATIONS

This article includes form declarations for each state in which one has been suggested by statute. If you travel widely or if you are likely to receive medical care in states other than the state in which you reside, fill out and sign appropriate form declarations for each state. There is no legal reason to limit the number of forms you sign. Do not be concerned if the various forms do not agree with each other because the only necessary form is the one which corresponds to the state in which you receive care.

EXECUTION FORMALITIES

States vary greatly with regard to signing formalities, especially when it comes to the qualification of witnesses. In order to make the Comprehensive Living Will valid in as many states as possible, the signing formalities in the Form are more extensive than required in any single state. While simplicity is desirable, the extra effort put into drafting and signing the comprehensive Living Will is warranted so as to insure that it will not be voided because of a procedural problem.

To avoid such problems, the Comprehensive Living Will Form suggests three witnesses (in case one would not qualify in any state). Confirmation by a notary public is recommended, though it is required in only a few states. In addition, as required in many states, the witnesses are asked to make a statement (referred to as an affidavit) declaring that they have no particular relationships with the declarant. (NOTE: In South Carolina the witness cannot be a physician.)

It is also directed that signatures be made in colored ink and the whole document only copied on a black-and-white copier to differentiate the original from a copy. This direction is important because an intact original serves as proof of the fact that the declaration has not been revoked.

1. Number and initial all pages up to and including any form document(s) in Article Eleventh which are to be part of the Comprehensive Living Will Declaration. Place the total number of pages in the blank as indicated in the paragraph beginning "In Witness Whereof," first in script and then write that number in the following parentheses. Do the same in the next paragraph.
2. Fill in the date, time, place, and your name as indicated on the Form.
3. Be sure to sign in the indicated position in colored ink. If you are unable to sign and someone else is signing for you, your name should be written first, then make a slash (/), and then have the person signing for you sign their own name. Print or type in the names as indicated.
4. The three witnesses should sign where indicated and include town or city of residence. They should carefully read the affidavit to make sure that it is accurate before signing.
5. Fill in the name of the state, county, town or city, and date at the top of the affidavit.
6. Fill in the rest of the affidavit as indicated before a notary public and have the notary public notarize the total document. This step will require the notary to fill in appropriate wording for your particular state.
7. After making appropriate copies, staple the total document together including any additional Living Will forms from other states. If these additional forms were signed before a notary, they should be placed after Article Tenth. If they were signed at a later date (as long as they are signed and witnessed as required by that state), they can be added to the back of the original Comprehensive Living Will Declaration.

AUTHOR'S ADVISORY

Writing a Living Will is a difficult, soul-searching experience. You should carefully consider all issues when writing such a Living Will.

One last suggestion—you should notify several people that you have prepared a Living Will so that attending physicians will be aware that it exists. You should distribute copies to physicians, family members, and designated proxies. When distributing copies, the location of the original (signed in colored ink) should also be noted because it is only the presence of an intact signed original that proves the continued validity of the document. In fact, holders of copies should seek the original before honoring the directives.

It is advisable that the instructional materials be left with the original signed Living Will to verify to others the process you went through in writing your Living Will.

COMPREHENSIVE LIVING WILL FORM DECLARATION

NOTICE TO DECLARANT

Before executing this document, you should be aware of the following:

1. This document gives your family and health-care providers guidance as to the kinds of medical treatment you would want under specific medical circumstances if, and only if, you are no longer able to make decisions for yourself. Directives made herein also serve as a legal means of assuring that your wishes will be honored. If you desire, you may also designate a proxy to make additional health-care decisions on your behalf, and you may state whether you do or do not want to receive any treatment.

2. If you designate a health-care proxy, that person should act in conformity with your wishes as herein expressed. If you should fail to express your wishes with regard to a particular circumstance herein, your proxy should first make decisions in accordance with his or her prior knowledge of your beliefs, and, in the absence of such knowledge, should then act in your best interests. If you choose not to name a proxy, your health-care providers will have a similar duty to act consistently with your instruction herein, but they will not be empowered to act if you have not left directives covering the clinical situation as it develops. Health-care providers who follow your directives in good faith are herein provided immunity from claims of malpractice or professional misconduct for so doing. It is wise to discuss your desires and beliefs with a proposed designated health-care proxy and with your physician to be sure they do not have any personal conflict with your directives.

3. This document will remain in effect until you amend or revoke it. Review it periodically to make sure it continues to reflect your preferences. To assure others that your wishes have not changed, re-date and sign the document periodically even though doing so is no longer required to maintain the document's validity, except in California. To revoke the declaration, deface the original copy and notify all designated health-care proxies, if any. A signed statement amending or revoking the document or direct notification to your health-care provider are alternative legal means of amending or revoking the document; the most certain method is to deface the original document by crossing out the front sheet and signature pages, writing on the signature page "I revoke," and signing. If the original document is not defaced, there is always the possibility that a treating physician may be shown the original document without being told it had been revoked by other means.

4. If you name a proxy, he or she will be given the same right as you have to examine your medical records and to consent to their disclosure to others unless you limit this right in the declaration.

5. Article Tenth of this Form allows you to express special thoughts in your own words if the provided form fails adequately to cover your concerns. Except for the statutory form declarations found in Article Eleventh, your personal desires can be added to the document by writing in the margins of the Form or by crossing out and initialing any parts of the Form you do not want included. These changes are best made in colored ink.

6. If there is anything in this document you do not understand, ask for professional help from a physician or attorney.

COMPREHENSIVE LIVING WILL DECLARATION
OF

_____
[Name in Caps]

I, _____, with a present address of
[Name]

_____, _____, _____,
[Address]   [Town or City]   [State]

after due consideration and being of sound mind, do make, publish, and declare this Comprehensive Living Will Declaration, hereby revoking any previous Living Will made by me.

_____
INITIALS

ARTICLE FIRST: PERSONAL STATEMENT REGARDING THE COMPREHENSIVE LIVING WILL

I am aware of the legal strengths and limitations of Living Wills and that they serve as evidence of my desires even when their legality is not guaranteed under a Living Will statute.

I therefore make the provisions included in this document for multiple reasons, but most particularly to give "clear and convincing" evidence of my desires to my physicians, family, a court, or any other person or facility responsible for my care so they shall not have to question what I would choose for myself if I were still able to decide. By so doing I also hope to prevent any guilt which could be inflicted on those who might be forced to make decisions for me without adequate guidance as to my wishes.

By recognizing the social goals, I do not want to diminish the legal aspects of this document. As an individual I am entitled to the right of self-determination in health care under the common law right of informed consent and the constitutional right to privacy in addition to rights granted by state statutes. This right is not negated if I become incompetent. I therefore demand that the directives contained herein be respected by my physicians, family, and the courts to the full extent possible under the existing jurisdictional law at any time that I shall be unable to make such decisions for myself as if they were my own decisions made at that time.

By making the following directives, I do not imply that I value life any less than anyone else, I only imply that I do not fear death itself as much as the indignities of deterioration, dependence, and/or hopeless pain. I do not fear suffering if after a period of such suffering there is a chance I would return to meaningful life. When this chance does not exist, however, I see no reason for suffering or making others suffer through my misfortunes. I believe that a life of unconsciousness, or pain, or a life in which I can not communicate is more akin to death than to life and wish my medical care be determined accordingly.

This Comprehensive Living Will Document is structured to make full use of the rights afforded me under both statutory and common law. It should be honored as follows:

Article Second shall be followed if I am in a condition which qualifies as "terminal" under the statute of the state in which I am receiving care and (a) I have executed the appropriate form in Article Eleventh or (b) my directive in Article Second can be substituted for the state declaration.

Article Third shall be followed as a common law directive if I am in a condition which does not qualify as terminal under the state's statutory definition but would under the state's common law using the broader definition contained therein.

Article Fourth shall be followed if I am in a state of permanent unconsciousness and such condition does not qualify as a terminal condition under the state's statutory definition.

The provisions of Article Fifth shall also apply if Article Second, Third, or Fourth is applicable.

I may or may not leave a directive in Article Sixth. If I do, provisions in this article should be followed if I suffer from end-stage dementia as defined therein.

If I complete Article Seventh, I have been diagnosed as suffering from a chronic, progressive, irreversible condition, and I want to leave specific directions regarding my future care. Provisions therein should be followed if and when I am no longer able to make medical decisions for myself.

Article Eighth contains additional provisions which should be employed in conjunction with all of the previous articles.

If filled out, Article Ninth designates a health-care proxy to help interpret and enforce my directives. If the state in which I am being treated does not recognize a health-care proxy, then such designation shall be interpreted to represent the designation of a durable power of attorney with the power to make health-care decisions, including the right to forsake life-support systems.

To the extent permitted under the law of the jurisdiction in which I am being treated, such designation shall also constitute the designation of a guardian or conservator of the person, or any similarly related fiduciary, as designated within that state.

I may not choose to burden any individual with these choices and will then rely solely on the good faith of my physician, family, or other fiduciary to honor the directives contained in this document. In either case, unless there exists significant new information which would have been likely to change my decisions, I expect my directives herein to determine the medical care I will receive.

Directives in Article Tenth should be incorporated into other directives as appropriate.

Article Eleventh includes signed documents conforming to state statutory law. These documents are included to invoke my statutory rights when possible because they may be considered more legally binding by those who must honor my directives. If I execute more than one Living Will form, the appropriate one should be used depending on the state in which I am receiving care.

I have purposely executed this Living Will Declaration with greater formality than required in most states out of a desire to maintain its validity in any state in which I am receiving care.

ARTICLE SECOND: STATUTORY TERMINAL CONDITION

The directive in this article shall be operative if the time comes when my attending physician determines (a) I am no longer competent to make or communicate decisions regarding my own medical care and (b) I am in a terminal medical condition as defined in a Living Will statute in the state in which I am receiving treatment. (**Initial within the parenthesis, sign, and enter name in either II(A)(1) or II(A)(2), not both. Cross out alternative paragraph.**)

II(A)(1)(   ). If I am incompetent and this paragraph II(A)(1) is initialed, I, _____, direct that if I
                              (**Sign above line. Print name here:** _____)
should have a terminal medical condition that would qualify me as terminal under the state Living Will statute, then life-support systems should be withheld or withdrawn, and I should be allowed to die unless there is a reasonable chance that use of such life-support systems will allow me to return to a meaningful life.

_____
INITIALS

II(A)(2)( ). If this paragraph II(A)(2) is initialed, I, _____, direct that my life should be
(Sign above line. Print name here: _____)
prolonged to the greatest extent reasonably possible through the use of life-support systems even if I am in a terminal condition.

II(B). If an appropriately signed and witnessed form declaration for the state in which I am being treated is a part of Article Eleventh of this Declaration and I would be qualified under that declaration, then that state declaration shall be substituted for the initialed and signed statement in II(A)(1) above.

II(C). If under the statute of the state in which I am being treated additional steps can be taken to qualify me as a terminal patient, I direct those caring for me to take such additional steps as are required so that I may benefit from the rights granted under the state statute.

II(D). If I would qualify as suffering from a terminal condition under the state statute but I have not signed an appropriate state form in Article Eleventh, I direct my physicians to substitute the above directive if permitted by the state statute.

ARTICLE THIRD: NON-STATUTORY TERMINAL CONDITION

The directive in this article shall be operative if the time comes when my attending physician determines (a) I am no longer competent to make or communicate decisions regarding my own medical care and (b) I am in a terminal medical condition, as defined below, but not under the definition of a Living Will statute in the state in which I am receiving treatment. This article shall not apply if my incompetency is due to a dementia, in which case Article Sixth shall apply.

(Initial within the parenthesis, sign, and enter name in either III(A)(1) or III(A)(2), not both. Cross out alternative paragraph.)

III(A)(1)( ). If I am incompetent and this paragraph III(A)(1) is initialed, I,_____, direct that if I
(Sign above line. Print name here: _____)
should have a terminal medical condition as defined in III(B) below, life-support systems be withheld or withdrawn and I be allowed to die and not be kept alive through their use.

III(A)(2)( ). If this paragraph III(A)(2) is initialed, I, _____, direct that my life should be prolonged
(Sign above line. Print name here: _____)
to the greatest extent reasonably possible through the use of life-support systems even if I am in a terminal condition as defined in III(B) below.

III(B). In making the determination of a terminal condition under this Article Third, I direct that my physicians employ the following definition:

"Terminal condition" means an incurable or irreversible medical condition which, within reasonable medical judgment (1) would produce the patient's death without the application of life-support systems **and** (2) even with the use of life-support systems, precludes the patient from (a) ever returning to competency **or** (b) ever returning to competency without unacceptable pain.

III(C). I recognize that this article may become applicable either because there is no Living Will statute in the state in which I am being treated or because the existing statute unduly narrows the definition of a terminal condition. I further recognize that in either case my directive herein will be legally supported only by my common law rights which include the right to continue to control my own medical care through written directives even if I am no longer competent to make decisions or speak for myself.

ARTICLE FOURTH: PERMANENT UNCONSCIOUSNESS

The directives in this article shall be operative if the time comes when my attending physician has determined that (a) I am no longer competent to make or communicate decisions regarding my own medical care and (b) I am permanently unconscious, as defined below, but am not terminal under the definition of a Living Will statute in the jurisdiction in which I am receiving treatment.

(Initial within the parenthesis, sign, and enter name in either IV(A)(1) or IV(A)(2), not both. Cross out alternative paragraph.)

IV(A)(1)( ). If I am incompetent and this paragraph IV(A)(1) is initialed, I, _____, direct that life-
(Sign above line. Print name here:_____)
support systems be withheld or withdrawn and I be allowed to die and not be kept alive through their use if I am permanently unconscious as defined in IV(B)(1) below.

IV(A)(2)( ). If this paragraph IV(A)(2) is initialed, I,_____, direct that my life should be prolonged to
(Sign above line. Print name here: _____)
the greatest extent reasonably possible through the use of life-support systems even if I am permanently unconscious as defined in IV(B)(1) below.

IV(B)(1). In making the determination of permanently unconscious under this Article Fourth, I direct that my physicians employ the following definition:

"Permanently unconscious" means a condition of irreversible coma or a persistent vegetative state in which, after appropriate medical evaluation, the attending physician and two physicians trained as neurologists or neuro-surgeons certify that there is no reasonable chance that I will ever recover the ability to perceive, think, remember, or engage in integrative thought involving self and the environment.

(Initial within the following parenthesis after IV(B)(2) if you desire that physicians wait a specific length of time before determining that you are permanently unconscious. The numbers suggested in the provision can be changed if you desire. If this is done, initial the changes. If you do not wish to specify a waiting time, cross out this entire paragraph IV(B)(2) and initial alongside.)

IV(B)(2)(   ). If this paragraph is initialed, I ask that my attending and consulting physicians wait the following periods of time before determining that I am "permanently unconscious."

    a. If I am over fifty (50) years of age, six (6) months.
    b. If I am twenty-five (25) to fifty (50) years of age, twelve (12) months.
    c. If I am under twenty-five (25) years of age, eighteen (18) months.

IV(C). I recognize that this article may become applicable either because there is no Living Will statute in the state in which I am being treated or because the existing statute does not recognize my condition as being terminal. I further recognize that in either case my directive herein will be legally supported solely by my common law right of self-determination in health care, which gives me the right to continue to control my own medical care through written directives even if I am no longer competent to make or communicate such decisions for myself.

ARTICLE FIFTH: ADDITIONAL DIRECTIVES/ARTICLES SECOND THROUGH FOURTH

The following directives shall apply if any of Articles Two, Three, or Four are operative.
    V(A). I direct that under Articles Second, Third, and Fourth the term "life-support system," or similar term, shall include not only mechanical or other artificial means to sustain, restore, or supplant a spontaneous vital function, but shall also include the following initialed items:
(Initial within parenthesis all types of medical care you do *not* want used under Articles Second through Fourth. If you would want some of these forms of care to still be employed, cross them out and initial alongside, not within the parenthesis.)

    (   ) transfusions, antibiotics, cardio-vascular regulators, cancer chemotherapeutics, anti-inflammatory medication, or any other drugs administered to control a disease process;
    (   ) nutrition and/or hydration given intravenously, by nasogastric or gastrostomy tube or any other means other than voluntarily taken by mouth;
    (   ) cardio-pulmonary resuscitation;
    (   ) surgery;
    (   ) invasive or investigational procedures, including intubation and needle punctures.

(Initial within the parenthesis, sign, and enter name below in V(B) only if you are a woman of childbearing age who wishes that life-support systems be withheld and withdrawn under Articles Second through Fourth even if you are pregnant.)
    V(B)(   ). If provision V(B) is initialed, I,_____, direct that if I am known to be pregnant, life-
        (Sign above line. Print name here: _____)
support systems shall still be withheld or withdrawn unless a medical evaluation determines the fetus is viable and could, with a reasonable degree of medical certainty, develop to live birth with continued application of such life-support systems.
    V(C). I direct that any requirement that I receive comfort care under any statute shall be limited to pain medication and such other therapy or procedure which clearly is required for my observable personal comfort, not the comfort of those around me.

ARTICLE SIXTH: END-STAGE DEMENTIA

(Preferably use in conjunction with a Designated Proxy in Article Ninth)
The directive in this article shall be operative if the time comes when my attending physician determines (a) I am no longer competent to make or communicate decisions regarding my own medical care and (b) I have been diagnosed as suffering from an "end-stage dementia" as defined in VI(B) below.
(Initial within the parenthesis, sign, and enter name in either VI(A)(1) or VI(A)(2), not both. Cross out alternative paragraph.)
    VI(A)(1)(   ). If this paragraph VI(A)(1) is initialed, I, _____, direct that life-support systems be
        (Sign above line. Print name here: _____)
withheld or withdrawn and I be allowed to die and not be kept alive through their use if my attending physician, a board certified psychiatrist, and a consulting neurologist or neuro-surgeon have all certified that I suffer from an end-stage dementia as defined in VI(B) below.
    VI(A)(2)(   ). If this paragraph VI(A)(2) is initialed, I,_____, direct that my life should be prolonged to
        (Sign above line. Print name here:_____)
the greatest extent reasonably possible through the use of life-support systems even if I have an end-stage dementia.
    VI(B). In making the determination of end-stage dementia under this Article Sixth, I direct that my physicians employ the following definition:
    "End-stage dementia" is an incurable *and* irreversible condition caused by injury, disease, or illness, including, but not limited to, Alzheimer's disease and multiple cerebro-vascular dementia, which prevents me from deriving pleasure from life because of the physical destruction of cognitive brain function.
    VI(C) (   ). If this paragraph VI(C) is initialed, I, _____, direct that life-support systems be withheld
        (Sign above line. Print name here: _____)
or withdrawn and I be allowed to die and not be kept alive through their use if my attending physician, and a consulting neurologist or neuro-surgeon have both certified that:

INITIALS

1. I have suffered one or more cerebro-vascular accident(s) which has/have left me significantly paralyzed in at least two limbs;
2. The chance of further recovery of physical function is minimal;
3. I am incapable of making medical decisions for myself;
4. The chance for further recovery of my mental function is minimal;
5. I have been told that medical care will be discontinued and have made no objection, nor have I indicated any desire for continued care; and
6. My designated proxy named in Article Ninth agrees I would not want to be kept alive in my present state with no significant hope of improvement.

VI(D). I direct that under this Article Sixth the term "life-support system," or similar term, shall include not only mechanical or other artificial means to sustain, restore, or supplant a spontaneous vital function, but shall also include the following initialed items:

(Initial within parenthesis all types of medical care you do *not* want used in case you suffer from an end-stage dementia. If you would want some of these forms of care still to be employed, cross them out and initial alongside, not within the parenthesis.)

(   ) transfusions, antibiotics, cardio-vascular regulators, cancer chemotherapeutics, anti-inflammatory medication, or any other drugs administered to control a disease process;

(   ) nutrition and/or hydration given intravenously, by nasogastric or gastrostomy tube or any other means other than voluntarily taken by mouth;

(   ) cardio-pulmonary resuscitation;

(   ) surgery;

(   ) invasive or investigational procedures, including intubation and needle punctures.

VI(E). I realize that some of the terms used in this article may be such that they are difficult to define objectively. For this reason I specifically direct that if I have appointed a health-care proxy in Article Ninth of this Living Will Declaration, his or her interpretation of such terms shall be held conclusive of my meaning and beseech my physicians, family, friends, guardians, and the administrators of any health-care facility in which I reside to honor my directives herein. In the absence of such a named proxy, I request my surrogate decision makers to act in good faith in following the most probable meaning of my directives.

ARTICLE SEVENTH: CHRONIC, PROGRESSIVE, IRREVERSIBLE CONDITION

(Preferably use in conjunction with a Designated Proxy in Article Ninth)
This Article Seventh shall only be made part of my Living Will Declaration if I have already been diagnosed as having a chronic, progressive, irreversible condition, and I want to preclude certain types of medical care in certain related situations in the future. The directives herein shall be subject to interpretation by any designated health-care proxy if named in Article Ninth below and shall only become operative if the time comes when my attending physician determines I am no longer competent to make or communicate decisions regarding my own medical care. Any directives in this article shall be additive to previous directives in this document.

VII(A). Statement: As of this date, _____, 19_____, I have been diagnosed by my physician, _____, M.D., as having the following disease or condition which I understand to be a chronic,
       [Name of Physician]
progressive, irreversible condition, even though progression may not be observable from day to day:

_____

At the present time I am competent to make my own health-care decisions on a day-to-day basis, but I fear that my condition or some intervening complication or condition shall make it impossible for me to direct such care either because of (1) mental incompetency or (2) the physical inability to insure that my directives are understood and given the consideration appropriate under the law.

I am particularly worried because I understand it is the nature of the disease or condition with which I am afflicted to produce or be complicated by a situation in which further medical care is only likely to prolong my death without the prospect of my ever returning to what I consider to be a meaningful life.

VII(B). I, _____, do therefore direct that life-support systems be withheld or
(Sign above line. Print name here: _____)
withdrawn and I be allowed to die and not be kept alive through their use if I am no longer competent to speak for myself and my attending physician and two additional physicians trained in an appropriate specialty determine there is no reasonable medical hope that use of such life-support systems would allow me to once again be able to enjoy my family, my surroundings, and/or my life.

VII(C). I direct that under this Article the term "life-support system," or similar term shall include not only mechanical or other artificial means to sustain, restore, or supplant a spontaneous vital function, but shall also include the following initialed items:

(Initial within parenthesis all types of medical care you do *not* want used in the treatment of the above named disease or condition or complications thereof if you are no longer able to decide for yourself. If you would want some of these forms of care to still be employed, cross them out and initial alongside, not within the parenthesis.)

(   ) transfusions, antibiotics, cardio-vascular regulators, cancer chemotherapeutics, anti-inflammatory medication, or any other drugs administered to control a disease process;

(   ) nutrition and/or hydration given intravenously, by nasogastric or gastrostomy tube or any other means other than voluntarily taken by mouth;

(   ) cardio-pulmonary resuscitation;

(   ) surgery;

(   ) invasive or investigational procedures, including intubation and needle punctures.

VII(D). I realize that some of the terms used in this article may be such that they are difficult to define objectively. For this reason I specifically direct that if I have appointed a health-care proxy in Article Ninth of this Living Will Declaration, his or her interpretation of such terms be held conclusive of my meaning and beseech my physicians, family, friends, guardians, and the administrators of any health-care facility in which I reside to honor my directives herein. In the absence of such a named proxy, I request my surrogate decision makers to act in good faith in following the most probable meaning of my directives.

ARTICLE EIGHTH: MISCELLANEOUS PROVISIONS

(Cross out any provision not desired.)
The following provisions shall apply to all directives within this Comprehensive Living Will Declaration:

VIII(A). All provisions in this document are severable and the invalidity of any such provision shall not affect the validity of any other provision.

VIII(B). Various jurisdictions at times will use different terms with essentially the same meaning. For instance, "life-support," "life-supporting," or "life-prolonging" are often used interchangeably. Other similar sets include "procedures/systems/treatments" and "condition/illness/disease." When any term is used in this document, I intend that such term be read as including any similar term which carries the same meaning or intent in the law of the jurisdiction in which I am being treated.

VIII(C). If I have previously executed a durable power of attorney, the directives and designated health-care proxy herein shall take precedence over any previously appointed attorney-in-fact with respect to health-care decisions. This Declaration shall have no effect on any nonhealth-care decision-making powers in such durable power of attorney.

VIII(D). The provisions herein shall not be invalidated by a statement in a standard will and testament revoking previous wills.

VIII(E). I do not intend any direct taking of my life, but only that my dying not be prolonged. Nevertheless, nothing in this document shall be interpreted to preclude my attending physician from undertaking medical or surgical treatment primarily intended for the relief of my pain or discomfort, even if such treatment should hasten the specific time to my death.

VIII(F). I hereby bind myself, my heirs, and any personal representatives to indemnify all participants in the making or honoring of these directives against any legal, professional, or social responsibility of any form.

VIII(G). If there shall be any procedural fault in the execution of this Living Will Declaration, my directives shall be followed to the full extent possible under the common law and corrected to the extent possible by consultation with my designated health-care proxy, if any.

VIII(H). I request that this document be given consideration equal to that of a regular will and testament distributing assets. Unless my health-care proxy or my attending physician can verify I have revoked this document orally or in writing, it should be held as valid upon presentation.

VIII(I). Purely to reassure physicians or my family of my ongoing belief in the directives contained herein, I may on occasion re-date and sign this document, but the absence of any such confirmation for any period of time shall have no effect on its legal validity any more than the absence of such confirmation would have on a regular will and testament.

VIII(J). If under the terms of these directives it would be appropriate to withhold life-support systems, I request that a letter to that effect be left at my bedside by the attending physician with a copy of this Living Will to inform any medical emergency personnel of the situation and to assure them all the immunity possible under the laws of the jurisdiction for following my directives in good faith.

VIII(K). I request that the holder of this Declaration or the holder of any copy of this Declaration carry the moral obligation to give such document to any physician in charge of my care who is not aware of its existence.

VIII(L). I do not wish to inflict any legal liability or mental anguish on any health-care provider who has served me during my life, but I do believe all such providers should carry the legal obligation to respect the expressed wishes of their patients. I therefore direct any health-care provider responsible for my care at a time when I am incompetent to speak for myself to act purely on medical evidence in making the decisions and taking the actions directed in this document. If for any personal reason or conviction this is not possible, I hold it as a personal obligation to me that such health-care provider transfer my care to another provider whose personal (or corporate) moral convictions would not interfere with honoring my directives.

ARTICLE NINTH: HEALTH-CARE PROXY DESIGNATION

(Preferred, especially if you include Article Sixth or Seventh)
IX(A). I hereby authorize my _____, _____,
                                          [Relationship]   [Name]
with present address of _____, _____, _____ as my health-care
                                          [Street]   [Town or City]   [State]

proxy, to implement my Comprehensive Living Will Declaration, and to accept direct responsibility for and/or refuse hospitalization and/or treatment on my behalf if I am incompetent to so act for myself.

In addition, I request that my health-care proxy be recognized as the individual responsible to act on my behalf in all health related matters, including, but not limited to, all of the following which are not crossed out and initialed within the parenthesis: **(Cross out and initial within parenthesis only those responsibilities you desire to be *excluded*.)**

(   ) serving as final decision maker regarding any uncertainties or ambiguities which may exist in or be related to this Declaration;

(   ) taking primary responsibility for making this document immediately known and available to any physician who is in charge of my care wherever that care is being given;

(   ) acting as the final arbiter of fact if any other person suggests I may have rescinded this document;

(   ) serving as the designated guardian or conservator of my person (or similar appointed fiduciary) if one is required;

(   ) accepting the responsibility to see that the physician and facilities involved in my care honor my directives herein to the full extent required under statutory or common law, which includes the right to transfer my care to alternative physicians or facilities, within or without the state; and/or

(   ) Deciding if I would have wanted life-support systems, including all those indicated in Article Fifth, withheld or withdrawn under circumstances not specifically covered by my Comprehensive Living Will Declaration.

IX(B). If the person I have named above refuses or is unable or unavailable to act on my behalf, or if I revoke that person's authority to act as my health-care proxy, I authorize as his or her replacement my _____,
                                                                            [Relationship]
_____, with present address of _____, _____, _____
      [Name]   [Street]   [Town or City]   [State]
to implement my Living Will Declaration as my substitute health-care proxy and to act in his or her stead and with the same powers conveyed.

If the two people I have named above refuse or are unable or unavailable to act on my behalf, or if I revoke their authority to act as my health-care proxy, I authorize as their replacement my _____, _____, with present
                                                      [Relationship]   [Name]
address of _____, _____, _____ to implement my Living Will Decla-
            [Street]   [Town or City]   [State]
ration as my substitute health-care proxy and to act in his or her stead and with the same powers conveyed.

(Cross out in ink the sections above for the designation of a substitute health-care proxy which have not been employed.)

IX(C). It is my intention that this appointment shall be honored by any alternative health-care proxies, my family, relatives, friends, physicians, attorneys, and in all court procedures as the final expression of my legal right to refuse medical or surgical treatment, and I accept the consequences of such a decision. I understand the full import of this designation of a health-care proxy, and I am emotionally and mentally competent to make this declaration.

IX(D). I understand that I have the right to revoke the appointment of the persons named above to act on my behalf at any time by communicating that decision to the proxy and/or my health-care provider. If that is my intention, I will cross out and initial this article in the original Living Will Declaration which can be identified because it is signed in colored ink.

ARTICLE TENTH: GUIDANCE PROVISIONS

For the benefit of any designated health-care proxy and those others who will be asked to conform my future medical care to my desires, I add the following expression of my beliefs to cover areas which I do not believe are adequately covered in the form document. If I am comfortable with the form provisions, the following will be left blank:

1. My directives forsaking medical care shall also apply under the following circumstances:

2. I particularly want to have all reasonable health care that may help in the following ways:

3. I particularly do not want the following:

4. I particularly want to have the following kinds of life-support systems employed if I am diagnosed to have a terminal condition:

5. I particularly want to have the following kinds of life-support systems employed if I am permanently unconscious:

———

INITIALS

6. I particularly do not want the following additional kinds of life-support systems employed if I am diagnosed to have a terminal condition:

7. I particularly do not want the following additional kinds of life-support systems employed if I am permanently unconscious:

8. I recognize that if I reject artificially administered nutrition and hydration, then I may die of dehydration or malnutrition rather than from my illness or injury. The following are any additional feelings and wishes regarding artificially administered sustenance:

9. Thoughts I feel are relevant to my instructions (you may, but need not, give your religious beliefs, philosophy, or other personal values that you feel are important; you may also state preferences concerning the location of your care or the physician or physicians who you would prefer direct your care):

ARTICLE ELEVENTH: STATE LIVING WILL FORM DECLARATIONS

Instructions

1. If your state has a Living Will form, cut out of book, complete form, and insert here.
2. If you wish to complete forms for several states, cut out of book, complete forms, and insert here.
3. If your state has no Living Will form and only observes common law, leave this section blank.

EXECUTION FORMALITIES

(**Number and initial all preceding pages including the form document in Article Eleventh, if any. Write in script the total number of pages in the blank as indicated below and then write that number in the parenthesis that follows. This number may be less than the page numbers if some articles are not included. Place these same numbers in the paragraph that follows the signatures. Then fill in the other blanks as indicated. If you later sign additional state declarations, attach them to the end of this document.**)

IN WITNESS WHEREOF, I have subscribed my name to this my LIVING WILL DECLARATION, with or without the designation of a HEALTH-CARE PROXY, consisting of this and the _____ (   ) preceding pages, and for
                                                                                                [Number of Pages]
the purpose of identification, I have initialed each such page, in the presence of the persons witnessing it at my request this
_____ day of _____, 199___, at _____ ___.m. at _____,
                                                                        [Time]   [Town or City]

_____.
                    [State]
[Sign in colored ink.]   _____
[Copy only in black.]
                                                      Typed (or Printed) Name of Declarant

                                                      _____
                                                      Typed (or Printed) Name of Person Signing for Declarant (if any)

    The forgoing instrument, consisting of this and the _____ (   ) preceding pages, was signed, published,
                                                                                    [Number of Pages]
and declared by _____, the Declarant, to be his/her Living Will Declaration, in our presence, and we,
                            [Name in Caps]
at his/her request, and in his/her presence and in the presence of each other have hereunto subscribed our names as witnesses
this _____ day of _____, 199___, at _____, _____.
                                                                                    [Town or City]   [State]

    WITNESSETH:
(**If this is an oral declaration being signed by someone other than the declarant, the person signing for the declarant should not be a witness.**)

_____
INITIALS

Witnesses sign here indicating their residency:

_____ residing at _____
                                                                 [Town or City/State]

_____ residing at _____
                                                                 [Town or City/State]

_____ residing at _____
                                                                 [Town or City/State]

(Witnesses [and party signing for oral declarant] shall also sign as follows in the form of an affidavit before a notary public:)

STATE OF   )
) ss: _____, _____, 199___
                                                        [Town or City]   [Month and Day]
COUNTY OF   )

Then and there personally appeared the within named

_____, _____, _____, and
    [First Witness]   [Second Witness]   [Third Witness]

_____ who being duly sworn, individually depose and attest that:
[Signer of Oral Declaration for Declarant, if any]

1. The declarant is personally known to them and they believe the declarant to be at least 18 years of age and of sound mind.
2. They are at least 18 years of age.
3. To the best of their knowledge, at the time of the execution of this Living Will Declaration, they:
   a. Are not related to the declarant by blood or marriage;
   b. Would not be entitled to any portion of the declarant's estate by any will or by operation of law under the rules of descent and distribution of this state;
   c. Are not the attending physician of declarant or an employee of the attending physician or an employee of the hospital or skilled nursing facility in which declarant is a patient;
   d. Are not directly financially responsible for the declarant's medical care; and
   e. Have no present claim against any portion of the estate of the declarant.
4. They witnessed the execution of the within Living Will Declaration by the within named declarant (or signer for an oral declarant).
5. The said declarant subscribed said Living Will Declaration and declared the same to be his/her Living Will in their presence.
6. They thereafter subscribed the same as witnesses in the presence of said declarant, and in the presence of each other and at the request of said declarant.
7. They make this affidavit at the request of the said declarant, _____.
                                                                              [Declarant's Name]

Witness 1: _____

Witness 2: _____

Witness 3: _____

Signer for Declarant, if any: _____

(Notary should place appropriate language here indicating the swearing to the above affidavit as is customary for the state in which the document is signed:)

Subscribed and sworn to before me   Seal:

this _____ day of _____, 199___.

_____
           [Notary Public]

(If the declaration is signed in a nursing home or other extended care facility, the additional witness designated below should sign below.)

I hereby witness this Living Will and attest that I believe the declarant to be of sound mind and to have made this Living Will Declaration willingly and voluntarily.

Witness _____*

* Medical director of skilled nursing facility or staff physician not participating in care of the patient or chief of the health-care facility.

_____
INITIALS

Section Eight

ALPHABETICAL LIST OF CASES DISCUSSED

A.B. *v* C.: *A.B.* v *C.*, 124 Misc. 2d 672, 477 N.Y.S.2d 281 (1984)

Barber: *Barber* v *Superior Court*, 147 Cal. App. 3d 1006, 195 Cal. Rptr. 484 (1983)

Barry: *Guardianship of Barry*, 445 So. 2d 465 (Fla. 2d Dist. Ct. App. 1984)

Bartling: *Bartling* v *Superior Court*, 163 Cal. App. 3d 186, 209 Cal. Rptr. 220 (2d Dist. Ct. App. 1984)

Bartling II: *Bartling* v *Glendale Adventist Med. Center*, 184 Cal. App. 3d 961, 229 Cal. Rptr. 360 (1986)

Blodgett: *In re Blodgett*, Washtenaw County Circuit Corut, Michigan, 83-26514-AZ (1983)

Bludworth: *John F. Kennedy Hospital* v *Bludworth*, 452 So. 2d 921 (Fla. 1984)

Botsford: *Union Pacific Railway Co.* v *Botsford*, 141 U.S. 250, 11 S.Ct 1000, 35 L.Ed. 734 (1891)

Bouvia: *Bouvia* v *County of Riverside*, Riverside County Superior Court (Cal.) Court No 159780 (1983)

Boyd: *In re Boyd*, 403 A.2d 744 (D.C. 1979)

Brophy: *Brophy* v *New England Mount Sinai Hospital*, 398 Mass. 417 (1986)

Browning: *In re Guardianship of Browning*, 543 So. 2d 258 (Fla. 2d Dist. Ct. App. 1989)

Caulk: *In re Caulk*, 125 N.H. 226, 480 A.2d 93 (1984)

Collins: *Collins* v *Davis*, 44 Misc. 2d 622, 254 N.Y.S.2d 666 (1964)

Colyer: *In re Welfare of Colyer*, 99 Wash. 2d 114, 660 P.2d 743 (1983)

Conroy: *In re Conroy*, 98 N.J. 321, 486 A.2d 1209 (1985)

Corbett: *Corbett* v *D'Alessandro*, 487 So. 2d 368 (Fla. 1986)

Crouse-Irving: *Crouse-Irving Mem. Hosp.* v *Paddock*, 127 Misc. 2d 101; 485 N.Y.S.2d 443 (1985)

Cruzan *v*
Harmon: *Cruzan* v *Harmon*, 760 S.W.2d 408. (Mo. 1988)

Cruzan *v*
Missouri: *Cruzan* v *Director, Missouri Department of Health*, 497 U.S. _____, 110 S.Ct. 2841, 111 L.Ed.2d 224 1990)

Culham: *In re Culham*, Oakland County Circuit Court 87-340537-AZ, Michigan (1987)

Delio: *Delio* v *Westchester County Medical Center*, 129 App. Civ. 2d 1, 516 N.Y.S. 2d 677 (1987)

Dinino: *Dinino* v *State*, 102 Wash. 2d 327, 684 P.2d 1297 (1984)

Drabick: *Conservatorship of Drabick*, 200 Cal. App. 3d 185, 245 Cal. Rptr. 840 (6th Dist. Ct. App. 1988)

Eichner: *Application of Eichner*, 102 Misc. 2d 184, 423 N.Y.S. 2d 580; mod 73 App. Div. 2d 431; 426 N.Y.S. 2d 517, mod 52 N.Y.S. 2d 363, 438 N.Y.S. 2d 266, 420 N.E.2d 64 (1979)

Farrell: *In re Farrell*, 108 N.J. 394, 529 A.2d 404 (1987)

Foody: *Foody* v *Manchester Memorial Hosp.*, 40 Conn. Supp. 127, 482 A.2d 713 (1984)

Foster: *Foster* v *Tourtellotte*, U.S. District Court No. CV81-5046 (CD Cal. 1981)

Gardner: *In re Gardner*, 534 A.2d 947 (Maine 1987)

George: *U.S.* v *George*, 239 F. Supp. 752 (D. Conn. 1965)

Golda Yoder: *In the Matter of Golda Yoder*, Cabell County Circuit Court, W. Virginia Civil No. 81-2690 (1981)

Grant: *In re Guardianship of Grant*, 109 Wash. 2d 545, 747 P.2d 445 (1987)

Hamlin: *In re Guardianship of Hamlin*, 102 Wash. 2df 810, 689 P.2d 1372 (1984)

Indian River
Mem. Hosp.: *Indian River Mem. Hospital & Schlamowitz* v *Cochran*, 19th Cir. Ct. of Fla. No. 85-334 (1985)

Jefferson: *Jefferson* v *Griffin-Spaulding County Hosp.*, 247 Ga. 86, 274 S.E.2d 457 (1981)

Jobes: *In re Jobes*, 108 N.J. 394, 529 A.2d 434 (1987)

Lane: *Lane* v *Candure*, 78 App. Ct. 588, 376 N.E.2d 1232 (Mass. 1987)

Leach: *Leach* v *Akron General Medical Center*, 68 Ohio Misc. 1, 426 N.E.2d 809 (1980)

L.H.R.: *In re L.H.R.*, 321 S.E.2d 716 (Ga. 1984)

Longeway: *In re Estate of Longeway* , 133 Ill. 2d 33 (1989)
Lydia Hall
 Hosp.:   *In re Lydia E. Hall Hospital*, 116 Misc. 2d 477, 455 N.Y.S.2d 706 (1982)
McAfee: *State* v *McAfee*, 259 Ga. 579, 385 S.E.2d 651 (1989)
McConnell: *McConnell* v *Beverly Enterprises-Connecticut Inc.*, 209 Conn. 692, 553 A.2d 596 (1989)
McVey: *McVey* v *Inglewood Hospital Asso.*, 216 N.J. Super. 502, 524 A.2d 450 (1987)
Morgan: *Morgan* v *Olds*, 417 N.W.2d 232 (Iowa Ct. App. 1987)
Morrison: *Conservatorship of Morrison*, 206 Cal. App. 3d 304, 253 Cal. Rptr. 530 (1st Dist. Ct. App. 1988)
Muhlenberg
 Hospital: *Muhlenberg Hospital* v *Paterson*, 128 N.J. Super. 498, 320 A.2d 518 (1974)
In re N.:   *In re N.*, 406 A.2d 1275 (D.C. 1979)
O'Conner: *In re Westchester County Medical Center on Behalf of O'Conner*, 72 N.Y.2d 517, 534 N.Y.S. 2d 886, 531
                           N.E.2d 607 (1988)
Peter: *In re Peter*, 108 N.J. 365, 529 A.2d 419 (1987)
Prange: *In re Prange*, 166 Ill. App. 3d 1091, 520 N.E.2d 946 (1st Dist. Ct. App. 1988)
President &
 Directors: *In re President & Directors of Georgetown College*, 531 F.2d 172 (D.C. Cir. 1964) (Wright, J. in chambers)
Quackenbush: *In re Quackenbush*, 156 N.J. Super. 282, 363 A.2d 785 (1978)
Quinlan: *In re Quinlan*, 70 N.J. 10, 355 A.2d 647 (1976)
Rasmussen: *Rasmussen* v *Fleming*, 154 Ariz. 207, 741 P.2d 674 (1987)
Requena: *In re Requena*, 213 N.J. Super. 475, 517 A.2d 886 (1936)
Robbins: *People* v *Robbins*, 83 App. Civ. 2d 271, 443 N.Y.S.2d 1016 (4th Dept. 1981)
Rodas: *In re Rodas*, Mesa County No. 86 PR 139 (Colo. Dist. Ct. 1987)
Roe: *Roe* v *Wade*, 410 U.S. 113, 93 S.Ct. 705, 35 L.Ed.2d 147 (1973)
Romeo: *Gray* v *Romeo*, 697 F. Supp. 580 (D.R.I. 1988)
Ross: *Ross* v *Hilltop*, 676 F. Supp. 1528 (D.Colo. 1987)
Saikewicz: *Superintendent of Belchertown State School* v *Saikewicz*, 373 Mass. 728, 370 N.E.2d 417 (1977)
Sanchez: *In re Sanchez*, 577 F. Supp. 7 (S.D.N.Y. 1983)
Satz: *Satz* v *Perlmutter*, 362 So. 2d 160 (Fla. 1978)
Schloendorff: *Schloendorff* v *Society of New York Hospital*, 211 N.Y. 125, 105 N.E. 92 (1914)
Severns: *In re Severns*, 425 A.2d 156 (Del. 1980)
Spring: *In re Spring*, 380 Mass. 629, 405 N.E.2d 115 (1980)
Storar: *Matter of Storar*, 52 N.Y.2d 363, 420 N.E.2d 64, 438 N.Y.S.2d 266 (1981)
Strachan: *Strachan* v *John F. Kennedy Memorial Hospital*, 209 N.J. Super. 300, 507 A.2d 718 (1986)
Torres: *In re Conservatorship of Torres*, 357 N.W.2d 332 (Minn. 1984)
Visbeck: *In re Visbeck*, 210 N.J. Super. 527, 510 A.2d 125 (1986)
Yetter: *In re Yetter*, 67 Pa.D.&C.2d 619 (1973)

Section Nine

THE LIVING WILL FORMS FOR 41 STATES (ALPHABETICALLY)

(SEE PAGE 161 FOR THE STATES WITHOUT LIVING WILL FORMS)

GUIDANCE FOR READERS

The following form declarations are taken from the statute of each state and should be attached as part of Article Eleventh in the Comprehensive Form Declaration advocated in this book. As previously mentioned, more than one form can and should be signed if the declarant is likely to receive medical care in more than one state. If more than one form is executed, each should be signed before the appropriate witnesses for that state as indicated on the top of each of the following state forms.

For the convenience of the reader, the section of the state statutes where the form can be found is noted at the top of each declaration form, as is the date of the last update of the statute available to the author at the time of the writing of this book. Copies of the state's statutes are likely to be present in most law offices, courts, or local libraries if the reader wishes to confirm that there have been no changes since this book was published.

Because form documents are widely distributed within the state, the wording of the form is seldom changed, except in conjunction with a major revision of the overall statute by the state legislature. In the last few years, this has most often occurred to allow directives to discontinue therapy when the declarant is in a persistent vegetative state and to permit directives to withhold nutrition and hydration. Because these changes only increase the coverage of the form declaration and do not limit previous directives, a Living Will employing an older form is likely to remain valid. If you wish to include the withholding of food and hydration or the withholding of care in case you are in the persistent vegetative state, it may be wise to check to see if there is a newer statutory form in your home state which covers these conditions, especially in states which require a declarant to use the exact form. In other states, the common law provisions in this book's suggested form should also be automatically valid if allowed under a newer statute.

Instructions for completing the Living Will form in each state are included before the specific declaration. As mentioned above, some states require that the exact form in the statute be employed, but most states suggest using the form substantially as written in the statute and then adding other directives if desired. Also noted is the presence or absence of a provision in the state statute which allows someone to sign for the declarant if the declarant is unable to sign for himself/herself.

States also vary with regard to provisions for designating a health care proxy as suggested in the Form Declaration in this book. Some provide a form for such a declaration within the state's recommended Living Will form, in which case the declarant would be wise to complete the section designating a proxy in the state as well as the designation of the proxy in the Form included in this book, making sure the designated proxies are the same. Other statutes suggest the designation of a proxy decision maker without providing a form, in which case the Form suggested in this book should be adequate alone.

States may also authorize the designation of a health care proxy as part of either a so-called "power of attorney for health care" or under the state's regular durable power of attorney act, but even if they fail to do so, it is likely that the designation of a proxy as advocated herein would still be held valid if it were ever questioned.

Remember, the requirements stated on these forms only relate to the part of the Living Will which falls under the statute. These regulations do not control the common law parts of the Living Will as suggested in the form in this book.

ALABAMA
1989; Health, Mental Health, Environmental Control §22-8A-4

A living will in the State of Alabama must be substantially in the form provided, but may include additional directives consistent with the suggested form. The declarant is specifically allowed to direct another person to sign the declaration on his or her behalf if unable to do so themselves. The living will statute neither provides for nor precludes the designation of a health care proxy.

A living will in the State of Alabama must be witnessed by two adults. The witnesses should not be

1) less than 19 years of age,
2) the person who signed the declaration for the declarant,
3) related to the declarant by blood or marriage,
4) a person who would inherit from the declarant under a will or codicil thereto or under the intestate laws of the state, or
5) financially responsible for the medical care of the declarant.

Declaration made this _____ day of _____ (month, year). I, _____, being of sound mind, willfully and voluntarily make known my desire that my dying shall not be artificially prolonged under the circumstances set forth below, do hereby declare:

If at any time I should have an incurable injury, disease, or illness certified to be a terminal condition by two physicians who have personally examined me, one of whom shall be my attending physician, and the physicians have determined that my death will occur whether or not life-sustaining procedures are utilized and where the application of life-sustaining procedures would serve only to artificially prolong the dying process, I direct that such procedures be withheld or withdrawn, and that I be permitted to die naturally with only the administration of medication or the performance of medical procedure deemed necessary to provide me with comfort care.

In the absence of my ability to give directions regarding the use of such life-sustaining procedures, it is my intention that this declaration shall be honored by my family and physician(s) as the final expression of my legal right to refuse medical or surgical treatment and accept the consequences from such refusal.

I understand the full import of this declaration and I am emotionally and mentally competent to make this declaration.

Signed _____

City, County, and State of Residence _____

_____

Date _____

The declarant has been personally known to me and I believe him or her to be of sound mind. I did not sign the declarant's signature above for or at the direction of the declarant. I am not related to the declarant by blood or marriage, entitled to any portion of the estate of the declarant according to the laws of intestate succession or under any will of declarant or codicil thereto, or directly financially responsible for declarant's medical care.

Witness _____

Witness _____

Date _____

ALASKA

1990; Health and Safety §18.12.070

A living will in the State of Alaska may, but need not, employ the form provided. The declarant is specifically allowed to direct another person to sign the declaration on his or her behalf if unable to do so themselves. The living will statute neither provides for nor precludes the designating of a health care proxy. The durable power of attorney statute specifically allows health care decisions, but does not specifically allow the agent to withhold or withdraw life support systems.

A living will in the State of Alaska should be witnessed by two adults or notarized by a notary public or a justice, judge, clerk, deputy clerk, or magistrate of a court of the State of Alaska or the United States, a United States postmaster, or certain commissioned officer authorized to acknowledge oaths.

The witnesses of the living will should not be

1) minors, or

2) related to the declarant by blood or marriage.

DECLARATION

If I should have an incurable or irreversible condition that will cause my death within a relatively short time, it is my desire that my life not be prolonged by administration of life-sustaining procedures.

If my condition is terminal and I am unable to participate in decisions regarding my medical treatment, I direct my attending physician to withhold or withdraw procedures that merely prolong the dying process and are not necessary to my comfort or to alleviate pain.

I [ ] do [ ] do not desire that nutrition or hydration (food and water) be provided by gastric tube or intravenously if necessary.

Signed this _____ day of _____, _____.

Signature _____

Place _____

The declarant is known to me and voluntarily signed or voluntarily directed another to sign this document in my presence.

Witness _____

Address _____

Witness _____

Address _____

State of _____

Judicial District _____

The foregoing instrument was acknowledged before me this (date) _____ by (name of person who acknowledged): _____.

_____

Signature of Person Taking Acknowledgment

_____

Title or Rank

_____

Serial Number, if any

THIS DECLARATION MUST BE EITHER WITNESSED BY TWO PERSONS OR ACKNOWLEDGED BY A PERSON QUALIFIED TO TAKE ACKNOWLEDGMENTS UNDER AS [Alaskan Statutes] §09.63.010.

ARIZONA

1991; Public Health and Safety §36-3202

A living will in the State of Arizona may, but need not be, in the form provided, but may include additional directives consistent with the suggested form. The declarant must sign the living will document him or herself. The living will statute neither provides for nor precludes the designating of a health care proxy.

A living will in the State of Arizona must be witnessed by two adults. The witnesses of the living will should not be

1) minors,

2) related to the declarant by blood or marriage,

3) a person who would inherit from the declarant under a will or codicil thereto or under the intestate laws of the state,

4) financially responsible for the medical care of the declarant, or

5) a person who has a claim against the declarant or would have a claim against the declarant's estate.

DECLARATION

Declaration made this _____ day of _____ (month, year). I, _____, being of sound mind, willfully and voluntarily make known my desire that my dying not be artificially prolonged under the circumstances set forth below and declare that:

If at any time I should have an incurable injury, disease, or illness certified to be a terminal condition by two physicians who have personally examined me, one of whom is my attending physician, and the physicians have determined that my death will occur unless life-sustaining procedures are used and if the application of life-sustaining procedures would serve only to artificially prolong the dying process, I direct that life-sustaining procedures be withheld or withdrawn and that I be permitted to die naturally with only the performance of medical procedures deemed necessary to provide me with comfort care.

I further direct that if at any time I should be in a permanent vegetative state or an irreversible coma as certified by two physicians who have personally examined me, one of whom is my attending physician, and the physicians determine that the application of life-sustaining procedures, including artificially administered food and fluids, will only artificially prolong my life in a permanent vegetative state or irreversible coma, I direct that these procedures, including the administration of food and fluids, be withheld or withdrawn and that I be permitted to die naturally with only the administration of medication to alleviate pain or the performance of other medical procedures necessary to provide me with comfort.

In the absence of my ability to give directions regarding the use of life-sustaining procedures, it is my intention that this declaration be honored by my family and attending physician as the final expression of my legal right to refuse medical or surgical treatment and accept the consequences from such refusal.

I understand the full import of this declaration and I have emotional and mental capacity to make this declaration.

Signed _____

City, County, and State of Residence _____

_____

    The declarant is personally known to me and I believe him to be of sound mind.

Witness _____

Witness _____

ARKANSAS

1989; Public Health and Welfare §20-17-202

A living will in the State of Arkansas may, but need not, employ the form provided. The declarant is specifically allowed to direct another person to sign the declaration on his or her behalf if unable to do so themselves. The living will statute specifically allows the delegation of a health care proxy, but does not provide a form to do so.

A living will in the State of Arkansas must be witnessed by two adults.

To cover terminal conditions:

DECLARATION

If I should have an incurable and irreversible condition that will cause my death within a relatively short time, and I am no longer able to make decisions regarding my medical treatment, I direct my attending physician, pursuant to the Arkansas Rights of the Terminally Ill or Permanently Unconscious Act, to [withhold or withdraw treatment that only prolongs the process of dying and is not necessary to my comfort or to alleviate pain] [follow the instructions of _____ whom I appoint as my Health Care Proxy to decide whether life-sustaining treatment should be withheld or withdrawn].

Signed this _____ day of _____, _____.

Signature _____

Address _____

The declarant voluntarily signed this writing in my presence.

Witness _____

Address _____

Witness _____

Address _____

To cover a situation in which the declarant is permanently unconscious add the following, choosing between bracketed language:

DECLARATION

If I should become permanently unconscious, I direct my attending physician, pursuant to the Arkansas Rights of the Terminally Ill or Permanently Unconscious Act, to [withhold or withdraw life-sustaining treatments that are no longer necessary to my comfort or to alleviate pain] [follow the instructions of _____ whom I appoint as my health care proxy to decide whether life-sustaining treatment should be withheld or withdrawn].

Signed this _____ day of _____, 19_____

Signature _____

Address _____

The declarant voluntarily signed this writing in my presence.

Witness _____

Address _____

Witness _____

Address _____

CALIFORNIA
1991; Health and Safety Code §71-88

A living will in the State of California must be precisely in the form provided. The declarant must sign the living will document him or herself. The living will statute neither provides for nor precludes the designating of a health care proxy, but provisions for the designation of a power of attorney for health care appear elsewhere in the California statutes.

A living will in the State of California must be witnessed by two adults. The witnesses of the living will should not be

1) minors,

2) related to the declarant by blood or marriage,

3) a person who would inherit from the declarant under a will or codicil thereto or under the intestate laws of the state,

4) a person who has a claim against the declarant or would have a claim against the declarant's estate,

5) the declarant's attending physician,

6) an employee of the declarant's attending physician,

7) or an employee of the health facility in which the declarant is being treated at the time of the signing of the living will document.

DIRECTIVE TO PHYSICIANS

Directive made this _____ day of _____ (month, year).

I, _____, being of sound mind, willfully and voluntarily make known my desire that my life shall not be artificially prolonged under the circumstances set forth below, do hereby declare:

1. If at any time I should have an incurable injury, disease, or illness certified to be a terminal condition by two physicians, and where the application of life-sustaining procedures would serve only to artificially prolong the moment of my death and where my physician determines that my death is imminent whether or not life-sustaining procedures are utilized, I direct that such procedures be withheld or withdrawn, and that I be permitted to die naturally.

2. In the absence of my ability to give directions regarding the use of such life-sustaining procedures, it is my intention that this directive shall be honored by my family and physician(s) as the final expression of my legal right to refuse medical or surgical treatment and accept the consequences from such refusal.

3. If I have been diagnosed as pregnant and that diagnosis is known to my physician, this directive shall have no force or effect during the course of my pregnancy.

4. I have been diagnosed and notified at least 14 days ago as having a terminal condition by _____, M.D., whose address is _____, and whose telephone number is _____. I understand that if I have not filled in the physician's name and address, it shall be presumed that I did not have a terminal condition when I made out this directive.

5. This directive shall have no force or effect five years from the date filled in above.

6. I understand the full import of this directive and I am emotionally and mentally competent to make this directive.

Signed _____

City, County, and State of Residence _____

The declarant has been personally known to me and I believe him or her to be of sound mind.

Witness _____

Witness _____

COLORADO
1990; Probate, Trusts & Fiduciaries §15-18-104

A living will in the State of Colorado may, but need not, employ the form provided. The declarant is specifically allowed to direct another person to sign the declaration on his or her behalf if unable to do so themselves. The living will statute neither provides for nor precludes the designating of a health care proxy. The durable power of attorney statute specifically allows health care decisions, but may or may not allow the withholding or withdrawal or life support systems.

A living will in the State of Colorado must be witnessed by two adults. The witnesses of the living will, or a party signing for the declarant, should not be

1) minors,

2) the person who signed the declaration for the declarant,

3) a person who would inherit from the declarant under a will or codicil thereto or under the intestate laws of the state,

4) a person who has a claim against the declarant or would have a claim against the declarant's estate.

5) the declarant's attending physician or any other physician,

6) an employee of the declarant's physician or the health care facility in which the declarant is being treated at the time of the signing of the living will document, or

7) a patient of a health care facility in which the declarant is a patient or resident.

DECLARATION AS TO MEDICAL OR SURGICAL TREATMENT

I, (name of declarant) _____, being of sound mind and at least eighteen years of age, direct that my life shall not be artificially prolonged under the circumstances set forth below and hereby declare that:

1. If at any time my attending physician and one other qualified physician certify in writing that:

   a. I have an injury, disease, or illness which is not curable or reversible and which, in their judgment, is a terminal condition, and

   b. For a period of seven consecutive days or more, I have been unconscious, comatose, or otherwise incompetent so as to be unable to make or communicate responsible decisions concerning my person, then

I direct that, in accordance with Colorado law, life-sustaining procedures shall be withdrawn and withheld pursuant to the terms of this declaration, it being understood that life-sustaining procedures shall not include any medical procedure or intervention for nourishment considered necessary by the attending physician to provide comfort or alleviate pain. However, I may specifically direct, in accordance with Colorado law, that artificial nourishment be withdrawn or withheld pursuant to the terms of this declaration.

2. In the event that the only procedure I am being provided is artificial nourishment, I direct that one of the following actions be taken:

(initials of declarant) _____ a. Artificial nourishment shall not be continued when it is the only procedure being provided; or (initials of declarant) _____ b. Artificial nourishment shall be continued for _____ days when it is the only procedure being provided; or

(initials of declarant) _____ c. Artificial nourishment shall be continued when it is the only procedure being provided.

3. I execute this declaration, as my free and voluntary act, this _____ day of _____, _____.

By: _____

Declarant

The foregoing instrument was signed and declared by _____ to be his declaration, in the presence of us, who, in his presence, in the presence of each other, and at his request, have signed our names below as witnesses, and we declare that, at the time of the execution of this instrument, the declarant, according to our best knowledge and belief, was of sound mind and under no constraint or undue influence.

Dated at _____, Colorado, this _____ day of _____, 19_____.

_____

Name and Address (Witness)

_____

Name and Address (Witness)

STATE OF COLORADO)
) ss.
County of   )

SUBSCRIBED and sworn to before me by _____, the declarant, and _____ and _____, witnesses, as the voluntary act and deed of the declarant this _____ day of _____, 19_____.

My commission expires:

_____

Notary Public

CONNECTICUT

1991; Public Act 91-283, replacing Health and Well-Being §19a-575

A living will in the State of Connecticut may, but need not, employ the form provided. The declarant must sign the living will document him or herself. The living will form provides for the designating of a health care proxy who may make the decision to withhold or withdraw life support systems. There is also a provision for the designation of a power of attorney for health care elsewhere in the Connecticut statutes, but it does not authorize the withholding or withdrawing of life support systems.

A living will in the State of Connecticut must be witnessed by two adults.

The witnesses of the living will should not be less than 18 years of age.

DOCUMENT CONCERNING WITHHOLDING OR WITHDRAWAL OF LIFE SUPPORT SYSTEMS

If the time comes when I am incapacitated to the point when I can no longer actively take part in decisions for my own life, and am unable to direct my physicians as to my own medical care, I wish this statement to stand as a testament of my wishes.

I, _____ (name), request that, if my condition is deemed terminal or if I am determined to be permanently unconscious, I be allowed to die and not be kept alive through life support systems. By terminal condition, I mean that I have an incurable or irreversible medical condition which, without the administration of life support systems, will, in the opinion of my attending physician, result in death within a relatively short time. By permanently unconscious I mean that I am in a permanent coma or persistent vegetative state which is an irreversible condition in which I am at no time aware of myself or the environment and show no behavioral response to the environment. The life support systems which I do not want include, but are not limited to:

Artificial respiration

Cardiopulmonary resuscitation

Artificial means of providing nutrition and hydration

(Cross out and initial life support systems you want administered)

I do not intend any direct taking of my life, but only that my dying not be unreasonably prolonged.

Other specific requests:

This request is made, after careful reflection, while I am of sound mind.

(Signature) _____

(Date) _____

This document was signed in our presence, by the above-named_____

(name) who appeared to be eighteen years of age or older, of sound mind, and able to understand the nature and consequences of health care decisions at the time the document was signed.

(Witness) _____

(Address) _____

(Witness) _____

(Address) _____

I appoint _____ (name) to be my Health Care Agent. If my attending physician determines that I am unable to understand and appreciate the nature and consequences of health care decisions and to reach and communicate an informed decision regarding treatment, my Health Care Agent is authorized to:

(1) Convey to my physician my wishes concerning the withholding or removal of life support systems.

(2) Take whatever actions are necessary to ensure that my wishes are given effect.

If this person is unwilling or unable to serve as my Health Care Agent, I appoint _____ _____ (name) to be my alternative Health Care Agent.

This request is made, after careful reflection, while I am of sound mind.

(Signature) _____

(Date) _____

This document was signed in our presence, by the above-named _____ (name) who appeared to be eighteen years of age or older, of sound mind, and able to understand the nature and consequences of health care decisions at the time the document was signed.

(Witness) _____

(Address) _____

(Witness) _____

(Address) _____

DELAWARE
1990; Health and Safety §25-03

A living will in the State of Delaware may employ any form favored by the declarant. The declarant is specifically allowed to direct another person to sign the declaration on his or her behalf if unable to do so themselves. The living will statute specifically allows the delegation of a health care proxy, but does not provide a form to do so.

A living will in the State of Delaware must be witnessed by two adults. The witnesses of the living will should not be

1) minors,

2) related to the declarant by blood or marriage,

3) a person who would inherit from the declarant under a will or codicil thereto or under the intestate laws of the state,

4) financially responsible for the medical care of the declarant,

5) a person who has a claim against the declarant or would have a claim against the declarant's estate, or

6) an employee of the hospital or health facility in which the declarant is being treated at the time of the signing of the living will document.

DISTRICT OF COLUMBIA

1990; Health and Safety §6-24-22

A living will in the District of Columbia must be substantially in the form provided, but may include additional directives consistent with the suggested form. The declarant is specifically allowed to direct another person to sign the declaration on his or her behalf if unable to do so themselves. The living will statute neither provides for nor precludes the designating of a health care proxy, but provisions for the designation of a power of attorney for health care appear elsewhere in the District of Columbia statutes.

A living will in the District of Columbia must be witnessed by two adults.

The witnesses of the living will should not be

1) less than 18 years of age,

2) the person who signed the declaration for the declarant,

3) related to the declarant by blood or marriage,

4) a person who would inherit from the declarant under a will or codicil thereto or under the intestate laws of the state,

5) financially responsible for the medical care of the declarant,

6) the declarant's attending physician,

7) an employee of the declarant's attending physician, or

8) an employee of the health facility in which the declarant is being treated at the time of the signing of the living will document.

DECLARATION

Declaration made this _____ day of _____ (month, year).

I, _____, being of sound mind, willfully and voluntarily make known my desires that my dying shall not be artificially prolonged under the circumstances set forth below, do declare:

If at any time I should have an incurable injury, disease, or illness certified to be a terminal condition by two physicians who have personally examined me, one of whom shall be my attending physician, and the physicians have determined that my death will occur whether or not life-sustaining procedures are utilized and where the application of life-sustaining procedures would serve only to artificially prolong the dying process, I direct that such procedures be withheld or withdrawn, and that I be permitted to die naturally with only the administration of medication or the performance of any medical procedure deemed necessary to provide me with comfort care or to alleviate pain.

In the absence of my ability to give directions regarding the use of such life-sustaining procedures, it is my intention that this declaration shall be honored by my family and physician(s) as the final expression of my legal right to refuse medical or surgical treatment and accept the consequences from such refusal.

I understand the full import of this declaration and I am emotionally and mentally competent to make this declaration.

Signed _____

Address _____

I believe the declarant to be of sound mind. I did not sign the declarant's signature above for or at the direction of the declarant. I am at least 18 years of age and am not related to the declarant by blood or marriage, entitled to any portion of the estate of the declarant according to the laws of intestate succession of the District of Columbia or under any will of the declarant or codicil thereto, or directly financially responsible for declarant's medical care. I am not the declarant's attending physician, an employee of the attending physician, or an employee of the health facility in which the declarant is a patient.

Witness _____

Witness _____

FLORIDA

1991; Civil Rights §765.05

A living will in the State of Florida may, but need not, employ the form provided. The declarant is specifically allowed to direct another person to sign the declaration on his or her behalf if unable to do so themselves. The living will statute specifically allows the delegation of a health care proxy, but does not provide a form to do so.

A living will in the State of Florida must be witnessed by two adults.

DECLARATION

Declaration made this _____ day of _____, 19_____. I, _____, willfully and voluntarily make known my desire that my dying not be artificially prolonged under the circumstances set forth below, and I do hereby declare:

If at any time I should have a terminal condition and if my attending physician has determined that there can be no recovery from such condition and that my death is imminent, I direct that life-prolonging procedures be withheld or withdrawn when the application of such procedures would serve only to prolong artificially the process of dying, and that I be permitted to die naturally with only the administration of medication or the performance of any medical procedure deemed necessary to provide me with comfort care or to alleviate pain. I do ( ) I do not ( ) desire that nutrition and hydration (food and water) be withheld or withdrawn when the application of such procedures would serve only to prolong artificially the process of dying.

In the absence of my ability to give directions regarding the use of such life-prolonging procedures, it is my intention that this declaration be honored by my family and physician as the final expression of my legal right to refuse medical or surgical treatment and to accept the consequences for such refusal.

If I have been diagnosed as pregnant and that diagnosis is known to my physician, this declaration shall have no force or effect during the course of my pregnancy.

I understand the full import of this declaration, and I am emotionally and mentally competent to make this declaration.

(Signed) _____

The declarant is known to me, and I believe him or her to be of sound mind.

Witness _____

Witness _____

GEORGIA
1990; Health §31-32-3

A living will in the State of Georgia must be substantially in the form provided. The declarant must sign the living will document him or herself. The living will statute neither provides for nor precludes the designating of a health care proxy, but provisions for the designation of a power of attorney for health care appear elsewhere in the Georgia statutes.

A living will in the State of Georgia must be witnessed by two adults. The witnesses of the living will should not be

1) incompetent or minors,

2) related to the declarant by blood or marriage,

3) a person who would inherit from the declarant under a will or codicil thereto or under the intestate laws of the state,

4) financially responsible for the medical care of the declarant,

5) a person who has a claim against the declarant or would have a claim against the declarant's estate,

6) the declarant's attending physician,

7) an employee of the declarant's attending physician, or

8) an employee of the health facility in which the declarant is being treated at the time of the signing of the living will document.

In the State of Georgia, if the declarant is a patient in an extended care facility, the living will must also be signed by either the chief of the hospital medical staff or any physician on the medical staff who is not participating in the care of the patient.

LIVING WILL

Living will made this _____ day of _____ (month, year).

I, _____, being of sound mind, willfully and voluntarily make known my desire that my life shall not be prolonged under the circumstances set forth below and do declare:

1. If at any time I should have a terminal condition as defined in and established in accordance with the procedures set forth in paragraph (10) of Code Section 31-32-2 of the Official Code of Georgia Annotated, I direct that the application of life-sustaining procedures to my body be withheld or withdrawn and that I be permitted to die;

2. In the absence of my ability to give directions regarding the use of such life-sustaining procedures, it is my intention that this living will shall be honored by my family and physician(s) as the final expression of my legal right to refuse medical or surgical treatment and accept the consequences from such refusal;

3. I understand that I may revoke this living will at any time;

4. I understand the full import of this living will, and I am at least 18 years of age and am emotionally and mentally competent to make this living will; and

5. If I am female and I have been diagnosed as pregnant, this living will shall have no force and effect during the course of my pregnancy.

Signed _____

_____ (City), _____ (County), and

_____ (State of Residence).

I hereby witness this living will and attest that:

(1) The declarant is personally known to me and I believe the declarant to be at least 18 years of age and of sound mind;

(2) I am at least 18 years of age;

(3) To the best of my knowledge, at the time of the execution of this living will, I:

    (a) Am not related to the declarant by blood or marriage;

    (b) Would not be entitled to any portion of the declarant's estate by any will or by operation of law under the rules of descent and distribution of this state;

    (c) Am not the attending physician of declarant or an employee of the attending physician or an employee of the hospital or skilled nursing facility in which declarant is a patient;

    (d) Am not directly financially responsible for the declarant's medical care; and

    (e) Have no present claim against any portion of the estate of the declarant;

(4) Declarant has signed this document in my presence as above-instructed, on the date above first shown.

Witness _____

Address _____

Witness _____

Address _____

Additional witness required when living will is signed in a hospital or skilled nursing facility.

I hereby witness this living will and attest that I believe the declarant to be of sound mind and to have made this living will willingly and voluntarily.

Witness: _____

Medical director of skilled nursing facility or staff physician not participating in care of the patient or

chief of the hospital medical staff or staff physician not participating in care of the patient

HAWAII
1990; Health §327D-4

A living will in the State of Hawaii may, but need not, employ the form provided. The declarant is specifically allowed to direct another person to sign the declaration on his or her behalf if unable to do so themselves. The living will statute neither provides for nor precludes the designating of a health care proxy.

A living will in the State of Hawaii must be witnessed by two adults and notarized by a notary public. The witnesses of the living will should not be

1) less than 18 years of age,

2) related to the declarant by blood, marriage, or adoption,

3) the declarant's attending physician, or

4) an employee of the declarant's physician or the health care facility in which the declarant is being treated at the time of the signing of the living will document.

DECLARATION

A. Statement of Declarant

Declaration made this _____ day of _____ (month, year). I, _____, being of sound mind, willfully and voluntarily make known my desire that my dying shall not be artificially prolonged under the circumstances set forth below, and do hereby declare:

If at any time I should have an incurable or irreversible condition certified to be terminal by two physicians who have personally examined me, one of whom shall be my attending physician, and the physicians have determined that I am unable to make decisions concerning my medical treatment, and that without administration of life-sustaining treatment my death will occur in a relatively short time, and where the application of life-sustaining procedures would serve only to prolong artificially the dying process, I direct that such procedures be withheld or withdrawn, and that I be permitted to die naturally with only the administration of medication, nourishment, or fluids or the performance of any medical procedure deemed necessary to provide me with comfort or to alleviate pain.

In the absence of my ability to give directions regarding the use of such life-sustaining procedures, it is my intention that this declaration shall be honored by my family and physician(s) as the final expressions of my legal right to refuse medical or surgical treatment and accept the consequences from such refusal.

I understand the full import of this declaration and I am emotionally and mentally competent to make this declaration.

Signed _____

Address _____

B. Statement of Witnesses

I am at least 18 years of age and not related to the declarant by blood, marriage, or adoption; and not the attending physician, an employee of the attending physician, or an employee of the medical care facility in which the declarant is a patient.

The declarant is personally known to me and I believe the declarant to be of sound mind.

Witness _____

Address _____

Witness _____

Address _____

C. Notarization

Subscribed, sworn to, and acknowledged before me by _____,

the declarant, and subscribed and sworn to before me by _____ and

_____, witnesses, this _____ day of _____, 19_____.

(SEAL) Signed _____

_____

(Official capacity of officer)

IDAHO

1990; Health and Safety, §39-4504

A living will in the State of Idaho must be substantially in the form provided. The declarant must sign the living will document him or herself. The living will statute provides a form provision for the delegation of Power of Attorney for Health Care.

A living will in the State of Idaho must be witnessed by two adults.

A LIVING WILL

A Directive to Withhold or to Provide Treatment

To my family, my relatives, my friends, my physicians, my employers, and all others whom it may concern:

Directive made this _____ day of _____ 19_____. I,

_____ (name), being of sound mind, willfully and voluntarily make known my desire that my life shall not be prolonged artificially under the circumstances set forth below, do hereby declare:

1. If at any time I should have an incurable injury, disease, illness, or condition certified to be terminal by two medical doctors who have examined me, and where the application of life-sustaining procedures of any kind would serve only to prolong artificially the moment of my death, and where a medical doctor determines that my death is imminent, whether or not life-sustaining procedures are utilized, or I have been diagnosed as being in a persistent vegetative state, I direct that the following marked expression of my intent be followed and that I be permitted to die naturally, and that I receive any medical treatment or care that may be required to keep me free of pain or distress.

Check one box:

☐ If at any time I should become unable to communicate my instructions, then I direct that all medical treatment, care, and nutrition and hydration necessary to restore my health, sustain my life, and to abolish or alleviate pain or distress be provided to me. Nutrition and hydration shall not be withheld or withdrawn from me if I would die from malnutrition or dehydration rather than from my injury, disease, illness, or condition.

☐ If at any time I should become unable to communicate my instructions and where the application of life-sustaining procedures shall serve only to prolong artificially the moment of my death, I direct such procedures be withheld or withdrawn except for the administration of nutrition and hydration.

☐ If at any time I should become unable to communicate my instructions and where the application of artificial life-sustaining procedures shall serve only to prolong artificially the moment of death, I direct such procedures be withheld or withdrawn including withdrawal of the administration of nutrition and hydration.

2. In the absence of my ability to give directions regarding the use of life-sustaining procedures, I hereby appoint

_____ (name) currently residing at

_____, as my attorney-in-fact/proxy for the making of decisions relating to my health care in my place; and it is my intention that this appointment shall be honored by him/her, by my family, relatives, friends, physicians, and lawyer as the final expression of my legal right to refuse medical or surgical treatment; and I accept the consequences of such a decision. I have duly executed a Durable Power of Attorney for health care decisions on this date.

3. In the absence of my ability to give further directions regarding my treatment, including life-sustaining procedures, it is my intention that this directive shall be honored by my family and physicians as the final expression of my legal right to refuse or accept medical and surgical treatment, and I accept the consequences of such refusal.

4. If I have been diagnosed as pregnant and that diagnosis is known to any interested person, this directive shall have no force during the course of my pregnancy.

5. I understand the full importance of this directive and am emotionally and mentally competent to make this directive. No participant in the making of this directive or in its being carried into effect, whether it be a medical doctor, my spouse, a relative, friend, or any other person shall be held responsible in any way, legally, professionally, or socially, for complying with my directions.

Signed _____

City, County, and State of Residence _____

The declarant has been known to me personally and I believe him/her to be of sound mind.

Witness _____

Address _____

Witness _____

Address _____

ILLINOIS
1990; Probate §110½ Paragraph 703

A living will in the State of Illinois may, but need not, employ the form provided. The declarant must sign the living will document him or herself. The living will statute neither provides for nor precludes the designating of a health care proxy, but provisions for the designation of a power of attorney for health care appear elsewhere in the Illinois statutes.

A living will in the State of Illinois must be witnessed by two adults. The witnesses of the living will should not be

1) less than 18 years of age,

2) the person who signed the declaration for the declarant,

3) a person who would inherit from the declarant under a will or codicil thereto or under the intestate laws of the state, or

4) financially responsible for the medical care of the declarant.

DECLARATION

This declaration is made this _____ day of _____ (month, year). I, _____, being of sound mind, willfully and voluntarily make known my desires that my moment of death shall not be artificially postponed.

If at any time I should have an incurable and irreversible injury, disease, or illness judged to be a terminal condition by my attending physician who has personally examined me and has determined that my death is imminent except for death delaying procedures, I direct that such procedures which would only prolong the dying process be withheld or withdrawn, and that I be permitted to die naturally with only the administration of medication, sustenance, or the performance of any medical procedure deemed necessary by my attending physician to provide me with comfort care.

In the absence of my ability to give directions regarding the use of such death delaying procedures, it is my intention that this declaration shall be honored by my family and physician as the final expression of my legal right to refuse medical or surgical treatment and accept the consequences from such refusal.

Signed _____

City, County, and State of Residence _____

The declarant is personally known to me and I believe him or her to be of sound mind. I saw the declarant sign the declaration in my presence (or the declarant acknowledged in my presence that he or she had signed the declaration) and I signed the declaration as a witness in the presence of the declarant. I did not sign the declarant's signature above for or at the direction of the declarant. At the date of this instrument, I am not entitled to any portion of the estate of the declarant according to the laws of intestate succession or, to the best of my knowledge and belief, under any will of declarant or other instrument taking effect at declarant's death, or directly financially responsible for declarant's medical care.

Witness _____

Witness _____

INDIANA
1990; Health and Hospitals §16-8-11-12

A living will in the State of Indiana must be substantially in the form provided, but may include additional directives consistent with the suggested form. The declarant is specifically allowed to direct another person to sign the declaration on his or her behalf if unable to do so themselves. The living will statute suggests that the declarant could designate a health care proxy to make health care decisions in the absence of a living will.

A living will in the State of Indiana must be witnessed by two competent adults. The witnesses of the living will should not be

1) less than 18 years of age,

2) the person who signed the declaration for the declarant,

3) a parent, spouse, or child of the declarant,

4) a person who would inherit from the declarant under a will or codicil thereto or under the intestate laws of the state, or

5) financially responsible for the medical care of the declarant.

LIVING WILL DECLARATION

Declaration made this _____ day of _____ (month, year). I, _____, being at least eighteen (18) years old and of sound mind, willfully and voluntarily make known my desires that my dying shall not be artificially prolonged under the circumstances set forth below, and I declare:

If at any time I have an incurable injury, disease, or illness certified in writing to be a terminal condition by my attending physician, and my attending physician has determined that my death will occur within a short period of time, and the use of life-prolonging procedures would serve only to artificially prolong the dying process, I direct that such procedures be withheld or withdrawn, and that I be permitted to die naturally with only the provision of appropriate nutrition and hydration and the administration of medication and the performance of any medical procedure necessary to provide me with comfort care or to alleviate pain.

In the absence of my ability to give directions regarding the use of life-prolonging procedures, it is my intention that this declaration be honored by my family and physician as the final expression of my legal right to refuse medical or surgical treatment and accept the consequences of the refusal.

I understand the full import of this declaration.

Signed _____

City, County, and State of Residence _____

The declarant has been personally known to me, and I believe (him/her) to be of sound mind. I did not sign the declarant's signature above for or at the direction of the declarant. I am not a parent, spouse, or child of the declarant. I am not entitled to any part of the declarant's estate or directly financially responsible for the declarant's medical care. I am competent and at least eighteen (18) years old.

Witness _____ Date _____

Witness _____ Date _____

IOWA
1991; Public Health §144A.3

A living will in the State of Iowa may, but need not, employ the form provided. The declarant is specifically allowed to direct another person to sign the declaration on his or her behalf if unable to do so themselves. The living will statute neither provides for nor precludes the designating of a health care proxy.

A living will in the State of Iowa must be witnessed by two adults.

DECLARATION

If I should have an incurable or irreversible condition that will cause my death within a relatively short time, it is my desire that my life not be prolonged by administration of life-sustaining procedures. If my condition is terminal and I am unable to participate in decisions regarding my medical treatment, I direct my attending physician to withhold or withdraw procedures that merely prolong the dying process and are not necessary to my comfort or freedom from pain.

Signed this _____ day of _____, _____

Signature _____

City, County, and State of Residence _____

The declarant is known to me and voluntarily signed this document in my presence.

Witness _____

Address _____

Witness _____

Address _____

KANSAS

1990; Public Health §65.28,103

A living will in the State of Kansas must be substantially in the form provided, but may include additional directives consistent with the suggested form. The declarant is specifically allowed to direct another person to sign the declaration on his or her behalf if unable to do so themselves. The living will statute neither provides for nor precludes the designating of a health care proxy, but provisions for the designation of a power of attorney for health care appear elsewhere in the Kansas statutes.

A living will in the State of Kansas must be witnessed by two adults. The witnesses of the living will should not be

1) less than 18 years of age,

2) the person who signed the declaration for the declarant,

3) related to the declarant by blood or marriage,

4) a person who would inherit from the declarant under a will or codicil thereto or under the intestate laws of the state, or

5) financially responsible for the medical care of the declarant.

DECLARATION

Declaration made this _____ day of _____ (month, year). I, _____, being of sound mind, willfully and voluntarily make known my desire that my dying shall not be artificially prolonged under the circumstances set forth below, do hereby declare:

If at any time I should have an incurable injury, disease, or illness certified to be a terminal condition by two physicians who have personally examined me, one of whom shall be my attending physician, and the physicians have determined that my death will occur whether or not life-sustaining procedures are utilized and where the application of life-sustaining procedures would serve only to artificially prolong the dying process, I direct that such procedures be withheld or withdrawn, and that I be permitted to die naturally with only the administration of medication or the performance of any medical procedure deemed necessary to provide me with comfort care.

In the absence of my ability to give directions regarding the use of such life-sustaining procedures, it is my intention that this declaration shall be honored by my family and physician(s) as the final expression of my legal right to refuse medical or surgical treatment and accept the consequences from such refusal.

I understand the full import of this declaration and I am emotionally and mentally competent to make this declaration.

Signed _____

City, County, and State of Residence _____

The declarant has been personally known to me and I believe him or her to be of sound mind. I did not sign the declarant's signature above for or at the direction of the declarant. I am not related to the declarant by blood or marriage, entitled to any portion of the estate of the declarant according to the laws of intestate succession or under any will of declarant or codicil thereto, or directly financially responsible for declarant's medical care.

Witness _____

Witness _____

KENTUCKY

1990; Occupations and Professions §311:626

A living will in the State of Kentucky must be substantially in the form provided, but may include additional directives consistent with the suggested form. The declarant must sign the document for him or herself. The living will statute neither provides for nor precludes the designating of a health care proxy, but provisions for the designation of a power of attorney for health care appear elsewhere in the Kentucky statutes.

A living will in the State of Kentucky must be witnessed by two adults. The witnesses of the living will should not be

1) less than 18 years of age,

2) a blood relative who would be a beneficiary of the declarant,

3) a person who would inherit from the declarant under a will or codicil thereto or under the intestate laws of the state,

4) the attending physician of the declarant or an employee of a health care facility in which the declarant is a patient, or

5) financially responsible for the medical care of the declarant.

DECLARATION

Declaration made this _____ day of _____ (month, year). I, _____, willfully and voluntarily make known my desire that my dying shall not be artificially prolonged under the circumstances set forth below, and do hereby declare:

If at any time I should have a terminal condition and my attending physician and one (1) other physician in their discretion, have determined such condition is incurable and irreversible and where the application of life-prolonging treatment would serve only to artificially prolong the dying process, I direct that such treatment be withheld or withdrawn, and that I be permitted to die naturally with only the administration of medication or the performance of any medical treatment deemed necessary to alleviate pain or for nutrition or hydration.

In the absence of my ability to give directions regarding the use of such life-prolonging treatment, it is my intention that this declaration shall be honored by my attending physician and family as the final expression of my legal right to refuse medical or surgical treatment and I accept the consequences of such refusal.

If I have been diagnosed as pregnant and that diagnosis is known to my attending physician, this directive shall have no force or effect during the course of my pregnancy.

I understand the full import of this declaration and I am emotionally and mentally competent to make this declaration.

Living Will Declarant _____

Witness _____

Witness _____

STATE OF KENTUCKY   )

)Sct.

COUNTY OF_____)

Before me, the undersigned authority, on this day personally appeared _____,
Living Will Declarant, and _____ and _____,
known to me to be witnesses whose names are each signed to the foregoing instrument, and all these persons being
first duly sworn, _____, Living Will Declarant, declare to me and to
the witnesses in my presence that the instrument is the Living Will Declaration of the declarant and that the
declarant has willingly signed and that such declarant executed it as a free and voluntary act for the purposes
therein expressed; and each of the witnesses stated to me, in the presence and hearing of the Living Will Declarant,
that the declarant signed the declaration as witness and to the best of such witness's knowledge, the Living Will
Declarant was eighteen (18) years of age or over, of sound mind, and under no constraint or undue influence.

Living Will Declarant _____

Witness _____

Address _____

Witness _____

Address _____

Subscribed, sworn to, and acknowledged before me by _____,
Living Will Declarant, and subscribed and sworn before me by _____,
and _____, witnesses, on this the _____ day of _____ (month, year).

Notary Public State at Large _____

Date my commission expires _____

LOUISIANA
1991; Public Health and Safety §40:1299.58.3

A living will in the State of Louisiana may, but need not, employ the form provided. The declarant is specifically allowed to direct another person to sign the declaration on his or her behalf if unable to do so themselves. The living will statute specifically allows the delegation of a health care proxy, but does not provide a form to do so.

A living will in the State of Louisiana must be witnessed by two adults.

DECLARATION

Declaration made this _____ day of _____ (month, year).

I, _____, being of sound mind, willfully and voluntarily make known my desire that my dying shall not be artificially prolonged under the circumstances set forth below and do hereby declare:

If at any time I should have an incurable injury, disease, or illness certified to be a terminal and irreversible condition by two physicians who have personally examined me, one of whom shall be my attending physician, and the physicians have determined that my death will occur whether or not life-sustaining procedures are utilized and where the application of life-sustaining procedures would serve only to prolong artificially the dying process, I direct that such procedures be withheld or withdrawn and that I be permitted to die naturally with only the administration of medication or the performance of any medical procedure deemed necessary to provide me with comfort care.

In the absence of my ability to give directions regarding the use of such life-sustaining procedures, it is my intention that this declaration shall be honored by my family and physician(s) as the final expression of my legal right to refuse medical or surgical treatment and accept the consequences from such refusal.

I understand the full import of this declaration and I am emotionally and mentally competent to make this declaration.

Signed _____

City, Parish, and State of Residence _____

The declarant has been personally known to me and I believe him or her to be of sound mind.

Witness _____

Witness _____

MAINE
1990; Human Services §18A-5-702,703

A living will in the State of Maine may, but need not, employ the form provided. The declarant is specifically allowed to direct another person to sign the declaration on his or her behalf if unable to do so themselves. The living will statute provides a form provision for the delegation of a health care proxy.

A living will in the State of Maine must be witnessed by two adults.

DECLARATION

If I should have an incurable and irreversible condition that, without the administration of life-sustaining treatment, will, in the opinion of my attending physician, cause my death within a relatively short time, and I am no longer able to make or communicate decisions regarding my medical treatment, I direct my attending physician, pursuant to the Uniform Rights of the Terminally Ill Act of this State, to withhold or withdraw such treatment that only prolongs the process of dying and is not necessary for my comfort or to alleviate pain.

Optional: I direct my attending physician to withhold or withdraw artificially administered nutrition and hydration that only prolongs the process of dying.

Signature _____

NOTE: This optional provision must be signed to be effective.

Signed this _____ day of _____, _____.

Signature _____

Address _____

Date of birth or social security number _____

The declarant voluntarily signed this writing in my presence.

Witness _____

Address _____

Witness _____

Address _____

NOTE: Maine law provides that artificially administered nutrition and hydration does not constitute a life-sustaining treatment that may be withheld or withdrawn pursuant to a living will declaration unless the declarant elects otherwise in the declaration itself.

If declarant is designating another individual to make decisions governing the withholding or withdrawal of life-sustaining treatment may, but need not, be in the following form:

DECLARATION

If I should have an incurable and irreversible condition that, without the administration of life-sustaining treatment, will, in the opinion of my attending physician, cause my death within a relatively short time, and I am no longer able to make or communicate decisions regarding my medical treatment, I appoint

_____ or, if my appointee is not reasonably available or is unwilling

to serve, _____, to make decisions on my behalf regarding with-

holding or withdrawal of such treatment that only prolongs the process of dying and is not necessary for my comfort

or to alleviate pain, pursuant to the Uniform Rights of the Terminally Ill Act of this State.

Optional: If the individual(s) I have so appointed is not reasonably available or is unwilling to serve, I direct

my attending physician, pursuant to the Uniform Rights of the Terminally Ill Act of this State, to withhold or

withdraw such treatment that only prolongs the process of dying and is not necessary for my comfort or to

alleviate pain.

    Signature _____

NOTE: This optional provision must be signed to be effective.

Optional: I direct my attending physician to withhold or withdraw artificially administered nutrition and

hydration that only prolongs the process of dying.

    Signature _____

NOTE: This optional provision must be signed to be effective.

Signed this _____ day of _____, _____.

Signature _____

Address _____

The declarant voluntarily signed this writing in my presence.

Witness _____

Address _____

Witness _____

Address _____

Name and address of designees.

Name _____

Address _____

NOTE: Maine law provides that artificially administered nutrition and hydration does not constitute a life-sustaining

treatment that may be withheld or withdrawn pursuant to a living will declaration unless the declarant elects

otherwise in the declaration itself.

MARYLAND
1990; Health-General §5-601

A living will in the State of Maryland must be substantially in the form provided, but may include additional directives consistent with the suggested form. The declarant is specifically allowed to direct another person to sign the declaration on his or her behalf if unable to do so themselves. The living will statute neither provides for nor precludes the designating of a health care proxy, but the durable power of attorney statute in Maryland has been held to allow the designation of an attorney-in-fact for health care decisions.

A living will in the State of Maryland must be witnessed by two adults. The witnesses of the living will should not be

1) less than 18 years of age,

2) the person who signed the declaration for the declarant,

3) related to the declarant by blood or marriage,

4) a person who would inherit from the declarant under a will or codicil thereto or under the intestate laws of the state,

5) financially responsible for the medical care of the declarant or an employee of any such person or institution, or

6) a person who has a claim against the declarant or would have a claim against the declarant's estate,

DECLARATION

On this _____ day of _____ (month, year), I,
_____, being of sound mind, willfully and voluntarily direct that my dying shall not be artificially prolonged under the circumstances set forth in this declaration:

If at any time I should have an incurable injury, disease, or illness certified to be a terminal condition by two (2) physicians who have personally examined me, one (1) of whom shall be my attending physician, and the physicians have determined that my death is imminent and will occur whether or not life-sustaining procedures are utilized and where the application of such procedures would serve only to artificially prolong the dying process, I direct that such procedures be withheld or withdrawn, and that I be permitted to die naturally with only the administration of medication, the administration of food and water, and the performance of any medical procedure that is necessary to provide comfort care or alleviate pain. In the absence of my ability to give directions regarding the use of such life-sustaining procedures, it is my intention that this declaration shall be honored by my family and physician(s) as the final expression of my right to control my medical care and treatment.

I am legally competent to make this declaration, and I understand its full import.

Signed _____

Address _____

_____

Under penalty of perjury, we state that this declaration was signed by _____ in the presence of the undersigned who, at _____ request, in _____ presence, and in the presence of each other, have hereunto signed our names as witnesses this _____ day of _____, 19_____. Further, each of us, individually, states that: The declarant is known to me, and I believe the declarant to be of sound mind. I did not sign the declarant's signature to this declaration. Based upon information and belief, I am not related to the declarant by blood or marriage, a creditor of the declarant, entitled to any portion of the estate of the declarant under any existing testamentary instrument of the declarant, entitled to any financial benefit by reason of the death of the declarant, financially or otherwise responsible for the declarant's medical care, nor an employee of any such person or institution.

_____

Address _____

_____

Address _____

MINNESOTA

1991; Adult Health Care Decisions; Statutes §145B.04

A living will in the State of Minnesota must be substantially in the form provided. The declarant is specifically allowed to direct another person to sign the declaration on his or her behalf if unable to do so themselves. The living will statute provides a form provision for the delegation of a health care proxy.

A living will in the State of Minnesota must be witnessed by two adults or notarized by a notary public. The witnesses of the living will or notary public should not be

1) minors,
2) a person who would inherit from the declarant under a will or codicil thereto or under the intestate laws of the state, or
3) the designated health care proxy.

HEALTH CARE DECLARATION

NOTICE:

This is an important legal document. Before signing this document, you should know these important facts:

(a) This document gives your health care providers or your designated proxy the power and guidance to make health care decisions according to your wishes when you are in a terminal condition and cannot do so. This document may include what kind of treatment you want or do not want and under what circumstances you want these decisions to be made. You may state where you want or do not want to receive any treatment.

(b) If you name a proxy in this document and that person agrees to serve as your proxy, that person has a duty to act consistently with your wishes. If the proxy does not know your wishes, the proxy has the duty to act in your best interests. If you do not name a proxy, your health care providers have a duty to act consistently with your instructions or tell you that they are unwilling to do so.

(c) This document will remain valid and in effect until and unless you amend or revoke it. Review this document periodically to make sure it continues to reflect your preferences. You may amend or revoke the declaration at any time by notifying your health care providers.

(d) Your named proxy has the same right as you have to examine your medical records and to consent to their disclosure for purposes related to your health care or insurance unless you limit this right in this document.

(e) If there is anything in this document that you do not understand, you should ask for professional help to have it explained to you.

TO MY FAMILY, DOCTORS, AND ALL THOSE CONCERNED WITH MY CARE:

I, _____, being an adult of sound mind, willfully and voluntarily make this statement as a directive to be followed if I am in a terminal condition and become unable to participate in decisions regarding my health care. I understand that my health care providers are legally bound to act consistently with my wishes, within the limits of reasonable medical practice and other applicable law. I also understand that I have the right to make medical and health care decisions for myself as long as I am able to do so and to revoke this declaration at any time.

(1) The following are my feelings and wishes regarding my health care (you may state the circumstances under which this declaration applies):

_____

_____

_____

_____

(2) I particularly want to have all appropriate health care that will help in the following ways (you may give instructions for care you do want):

_____

_____

_____

_____

(3) I particularly do not want the following (you may list specific treatment you do not want in certain circumstances):

_____

_____

(4) I particularly want to have the following kinds of life-sustaining treatment if I am diagnosed to have a terminal condition (you may list the specific types of life-sustaining treatment that you do want if you have a terminal condition):

_____

_____

_____

(5) I particularly do not want the following kinds of life-sustaining treatment if I am diagnosed to have a terminal condition (you may list the specific types of life-sustaining treatment that you do not want if you have a terminal condition):

_____
_____
_____

(6) I recognize that if I reject artificially administered sustenance, then I may die of dehydration or malnutrition rather than from my illness or injury. The following are my feelings and wishes regarding artificially administered sustenance should I have a terminal condition (you may indicate whether you wish to receive food and fluids given to you in some other way than by mouth if you have a terminal condition):

_____
_____
_____

(7) Thoughts I feel are relevant to my instructions. (You may, but need not, give your religious beliefs, philosophy, or other personal values that you feel are important. You may also state preferences concerning the location of your care.)

_____
_____
_____

(8) Proxy Designation. (If you wish, you may name someone to see that your wishes are carried out, but you do not have to do this. You may also name a proxy without including specific instructions regarding your care. If you name a proxy, you should discuss your wishes with that person.)

If I become unable to communicate my instructions, I designate the following person(s) to act on my behalf consistently with my instructions, if any, as stated in this document. Unless I write instructions that limit my proxy's authority, my proxy has full power and authority to make health care decisions for me. If a guardian or conservator of the person is to be appointed for me, I nominate my proxy named in this document to act as guardian or conservator of my person.

Name: _____

Address: _____

Phone Number: _____

Relationship (if any): _____

If the person I have named above refuses or is unable or unavailable to act on my behalf, or if I revoke that person's authority to act as my proxy, I authorize the following person to do so:

Name: _____

Address: _____

Phone Number: _____

Relationship (if any): _____

I understand that I have the right to revoke the appointment of the persons named above to act on my behalf at any time by communicating that decision to the proxy or my health care provider.

Date: _____

Signed: _____

State of _____

County of _____

Subscribed, sworn to, and acknowledged before me by _____ on this

_____ day of _____, 19_____.

Notary Public _____

or _____

(Sign and date here in the presence of two adult witnesses, neither of whom is entitled to any part of your estate under a will or by operation of law, and neither of whom is your proxy.)

I certify that the declarant voluntarily signed this declaration in my presence and that the declarant is personally known to me. I am not named as a proxy by the declaration, and to the best of my knowledge, I am not entitled to any part of the estate of the declarant under a will or by operation of law.

Witness _____ Address _____

Witness _____ Address _____

Reminder: Keep the signed original with your personal papers. Give signed copies to your doctors, family, and proxy.

MISSISSIPPI
1990; Public Health §41-41-107

A living will in the State of Mississippi must be substantially in the form provided. The declarant must sign the living will document him or herself. The living will statute neither provides for nor precludes the designating of a health care proxy, but provisions for the designation of a power of attorney for health care appear elsewhere in the Mississippi statutes.

A living will in the State of Mississippi must be witnessed by two adults. The witnesses of the living will should not be

1) minors,

2) related to the declarant by blood or marriage,

3) a person who would inherit from the declarant under a will or codicil thereto or under the intestate laws of the state,

4) the declarant's attending physician,

5) a person who has a claim against the declarant or would have a claim against the declarant's estate, or

6) an employee of the declarant's attending physician.

The declaration shall be filed with the bureau of vital statistics of the state board of health.

DECLARATION made on _____ (date) by _____ (person's name) of _____ (address), _____ (Social Security number).

I, _____, being of sound mind declare that if at any time I should suffer a terminal physical condition which causes me severe distress or unconsciousness, and my physician, with the concurrence of two (2) other physicians, believes that there is no expectation of my regaining consciousness or a state of health that is meaningful to me and but for the use of life-sustaining mechanisms my death would be imminent, I desire that the mechanisms be withdrawn so that I may die naturally. However, if I have been diagnosed as pregnant and that diagnosis is known to my physician, this declaration shall have no force or effect during the course of my pregnancy. I further declare that this declaration shall be honored by my family and my physician as the final expression of my desires concerning the manner in which I die.

Signed _____

I hereby witness this declaration and attest that:

(1) I personally know the Declarant and believe the Declarant to be of sound mind.

(2) To the best of my knowledge, at the time of the execution of this declaration, I:

(a) Am not related to the Declarant by blood or marriage,

(b) Do not have any claim on the estate of the Declarant,

(c) Am not entitled to any portion of the Declarant's estate by any will or by operation of law, and

(d) Am not a physician attending the Declarant or person employed by a physician attending the Declarant.

Witness _____

Address _____

Social Security Number _____

Witness _____

Address _____

Social Security Number _____

NOTE: The declaration shall be filed with the bureau of vital statistics of the state board of health.

MISSOURI
1991; Trust and Estates §459.015

A living will in the State of Missouri may, but need not, employ the form provided. The declarant is specifically allowed to direct another person to sign the declaration on his or her behalf if unable to do so themselves. The living will statute neither provides for nor precludes the designating of a health care proxy.

A living will in the State of Missouri must be witnessed by two adults.

DECLARATION

I have the primary right to make my own decisions concerning treatment that might unduly prolong the dying process. By this declaration I express to my physician, family, and friends my intent. If I should have a terminal condition it is my desire that my dying not be prolonged by administration of death-prolonging procedures. If my condition is terminal and I am unable to participate in decisions regarding my medical treatment, I direct my attending physician to withhold or withdraw medical procedures that merely prolong the dying process and are not necessary to my comfort or to alleviate pain. It is not my intent to authorize affirmative or deliberate acts or omissions to shorten my life rather only to permit the natural process of dying.

Signed this _____ day of _____

Signature _____

City, County, and State of Residence _____

The declarant is known to me, is eighteen years of age or older, of sound mind, and voluntarily signed this document in my presence.

Witness _____

Address _____

Witness _____

Address _____

REVOCATION PROVISION

I hereby revoke the above declaration.

Signed _____

(Signature of Declarant)

Date _____

MONTANA
1991 Rights of the Terminally Ill Act HB 0635

A living will in the State of Montana may, but need not, employ the form provided. The declarant is specifically allowed to direct another person to sign the declaration on his or her behalf if unable to do so themselves. The living will statute provides for designating of a health care proxy.

A living will in the State of Montana must be witnessed by two adults.

DECLARATION

If I should have an incurable or irreversible condition that, without the administration of life-sustaining treatment, will, in the opinion of my attending physician, cause my death within a relatively short time, and I am no longer able to make decisions regarding my medical treatment, I direct my attending physician, pursuant to the Montana Rights of the Terminally Ill Act, to withhold or withdraw treatment that only prolongs the process of dying and is not necessary to my comfort or to alleviate pain.

Signed this _____ day of _____, _____

Signature _____

City, County, and State of Residence _____

The declarant voluntarily signed this document in my presence.

Witness _____

Address _____

Witness _____

Address _____

DECLARATION

If I should have an incurable and irreversible condition that, without the administration of life-sustaining treatment, will, in the opinion of my attending physician, cause my death within a relatively short time and I am no longer able to make decisions regarding my medical treatment, I appoint _____ or, if he or she is not reasonably available or is unwilling to serve, _____, to make decisions on my behalf regarding withholding or withdrawal of treatment that only prolongs the process of dying and is not necessary for my comfort or to alleviate pain, pursuant to the Montana Rights of the Terminally Ill Act.

If the individual I have appointed is not reasonably available or is unwilling to serve, I direct my attending physician, pursuant to the Montana Rights of the Terminally Ill Act, to withhold or withdraw treatment that only prolongs the process of dying and is not necessary for my comfort or to alleviate pain.

Signed this _____ day of _____, _____

Signature _____

City, County, and State of Residence _____

The declarant voluntarily signed this document in my presence.

Witness _____

Address _____

Witness _____

Address _____

Name and address of designee.

Name _____

Address _____

NEVADA

1991; Uniform Act on Rights of the Terminally Ill

A living will in the State of Nevada may, but need not be, in the form provided. The declarant is specifically allowed to direct another person to sign the declaration on his or her behalf if unable to do so themselves. The living will statute provides for the designating of a health care proxy. Provisions for the designation of a power of attorney for health care appear elsewhere in the Nevada statutes.

A living will in the State of Nevada must be witnessed by two adults.

A copy should be placed in the declarant's medical records.

DECLARATION

If I should have an incurable and irreversible condition that, without the administration of life-sustaining treatment, will, in the opinion of my attending physician, cause my death within a relatively short time, and I am no longer able to make decisions regarding my medical treatment, I direct my attending physician, pursuant to NRS 449.540 to 449.690, inclusive, and sections 2 to 12 inclusive, of this act, to withhold or withdraw treatment that only prolongs the process of dying and is not necessary for my comfort or to alleviate pain.

If you wish to include this statement, you must INITIAL the statement in the box provided:

(If the statement reflects your desires, initial the box next to the statement.)

I direct my attending physician not to withhold or withdraw artificial nutrition and hydration by way of the gastro-intestinal tract if such a withholding or withdrawal would result in my death by starvation or dehydration. ☐

Signed this _____ day of _____, _____

Signature _____

Address _____

The declarant voluntarily signed this writing in my presence.

Witness _____

Address _____

Witness _____

Address _____

NEW HAMPSHIRE
1990; Public Health §137:H:3

A living will in the State of New Hampshire may, but need not, employ the form provided. The declarant must sign the living will document him or herself. The living will statute neither provides for nor precludes the designating of a health care proxy.

A living will in the State of New Hampshire must be witnessed by two adults and notarized by a notary public or justice of the peace or other official authorized to administer oaths in the place of execution. The witnesses of the living will should not be

1) minors,

2) spouse,

3) a person who would inherit from the declarant under a will or codicil thereto or under the intestate laws of the state,

4) a person who has a claim against the declarant or would have a claim against the declarant's estate,

5) the declarant's attending physician, or

6) anyone acting under the direction of the declarant's attending physician.

DECLARATION

Declaration made this _____ day of _____ (month, year). I,

_____, being of sound mind, willfully and voluntarily make known my desire that my dying shall not be artificially prolonged under the circumstances set forth below, do hereby declare:

If at any time I should have an incurable injury, disease, or illness certified to be a terminal condition by two physicians who have personally examined me, one of whom shall be my attending physician, and the physicians have determined that my death will occur whether or not life-sustaining procedures are utilized and where the application of life-sustaining procedures would serve only to artificially prolong the dying process, I direct that such procedures be withheld or withdrawn, and that I be permitted to die naturally with only the administration of medication, sustenance, or the performance of any medical procedure deemed necessary to provide me with comfort care.

In the absence of my ability to give directions regarding the use of such life-sustaining procedures, it is my intention that this declaration shall be honored by my family and physicians as the final expression of my right to refuse medical or surgical treatment and accept the consequences of such refusal.

I understand the full import of this declaration, and I am emotionally and mentally competent to make this declaration.

Signed _____

State of _____

County _____

We, the declarant and witnesses, being duly sworn each declare to the notary public or justice of the peace or other official signing below as follows:

1. The declarant signed the instrument as a free and voluntary act for the purposes expressed, or expressly directed another to sign for him.

2. Each witness signed at the request of the declarant, in his presence, and in the presence of the other witness.

3. To the best of my knowledge, at the time of the signing the declarant was at least 18 years of age, and was of sane mind and under no constraint or undue influence.

Declarant _____

Witness _____

Witness _____

The affidavit shall be made before a notary public or justice of the peace or other official authorized to administer oaths in the place of execution, who shall not also serve as a witness, and who shall complete and sign a certificate in content and form substantially as follows:

Sworn to and signed before me by _____, declarant,

_____ and _____,

witnesses on _____.

Signature _____

Official Capacity _____

NEW JERSEY
1991; Public Law, Chapter 201; Advance Directives for Health Care [Effective, mid-January, 1992]

The New Jersey statute provides for both a living will (called an "instruction directive" by the statute) and designation of a "health care representative" to make health care decisions. No forms are provided. The statute specifically allows the declaration to be signed by another at the direction of the declarant. The declaration must be signed and witnessed by two adults who are not the health care representative or may be signed before a witnessing notary public, attorney, or other individual authorized to administer oaths. The witnesses must attest that "the declarant is of sound mind and free of duress and undue influence."

NORTH CAROLINA
1990; Medicine and Allied Occupations §90-321

A living will in the State of North Carolina must be precisely in the form provided. The declarant must sign the living will document him or herself. The living will statute neither provides for nor precludes the designating of a health care proxy.

A living will in the State of North Carolina must be witnessed by two adults and notarized by a notary public or a similar official authorized to verify the signing of the declarant. The witnesses of the living will should not be

1) minors,

2) related to the declarant by blood or marriage,

3) a person who would inherit from the declarant under a will or codicil thereto or under the intestate laws of the state,

4) a person who has a claim against the declarant or would have a claim against the declarant's estate,

5) the declarant's attending physician, or

6) an employee of the declarant's physician or the health care facility, nursing home, or group-home in which the declarant is being treated at the time of the signing of the living will document.

DECLARATION OF A DESIRE FOR A NATURAL DEATH

I, _____, being of sound mind, desire that my life not be prolonged by extraordinary means if my condition is determined to be terminal and incurable. I am aware and understand that this writing authorizes a physician to withhold or discontinue extraordinary means.

This the _____ day of _____

Signature _____

I hereby state that the declarant, _____, being of sound mind signed the above declaration in my presence and that I am not related to the declarant by blood or marriage and that I do not know or have a reasonable expectation that I would be entitled to any portion of the estate of the declarant under any existing will or codicil of the declarant or as an heir under the Intestate Succession Act if the declarant died on this date without a will. I also state that I am not the declarant's attending physician or an employee of the declarant's attending physician or an employee of a health facility in which the declarant is a patient or an employee of a nursing home or any group-care home where the declarant resides. I further state that I do not now have any claim against the declarant.

Witness _____

Witness _____

The clerk or the assistant clerk, or a notary public may, upon proper proof, certify the declaration as follows:

CERTIFICATE

I, _____, Clerk (Assistant Clerk) of Superior Court or Notary Public (circle one as appropriate) for _____ County hereby certify that _____, the declarant, appeared before me and swore to me and to the witnesses in my presence that this instrument is his Declaration of a Desire for a Natural Death, and that he had willingly and voluntarily made and executed it as his free act and deed for the purposes expressed in it.

I further certify that _____ and _____, witnesses, appeared before me and swore that they witnessed _____, declarant, sign the attached declaration, believing him to be of sound mind; and also swore that at the time they witnessed the declaration (i) they were not related within the third degree to the declarant or to the declarant's spouse, and (ii) they did not know or have a reasonable expectation that they would be entitled to any portion of the estate of the declarant upon the declarant's death under any will of the declarant or codicil thereto then existing or under the Intestate Succession Act as it provides at that time, and (iii) they were not a physician attending the declarant or an employee of an attending physician or an employee of a health facility in which the declarant was a patient or an employee of a nursing home or any group-care home in which the declarant resided, and (iv) they did not have a claim against the declarant. I further certify that I am satisfied as to the genuineness and due execution of the declaration.

This the _____ day of _____

Clerk (Assistant Clerk) of Superior Court or Notary Public (circle one as appropriate) for the County of

_____

NORTH DAKOTA
1991; Health and Safety §23-06-4-03

A living will in the State of North Dakota must be substantially in the form provided, but may include additional directives consistent with the suggested form. The declarant is specifically allowed to direct another person to sign the declaration on his or her behalf if unable to do so themselves. The living will statute neither provides for nor precludes the designating of a health care proxy.

A living will in the State of North Dakota must be witnessed by two adults. The witnesses of the living will should not be

1) minors,

2) related to the declarant by blood or marriage,

3) a person who would inherit from the declarant under a will or codicil thereto or under the intestate laws of the state,

4) financially responsible for the medical care of the declarant,

5) a person who has a claim against the declarant or would have a claim against the declarant's estate, or

6) the declarant's attending physician.

In the State of North Dakota, if the declarant is a patient in a long-term care facility, one of the two witnesses to the declaration must be a recognized member of the clergy, an attorney licensed to practice in the state, or a person as may be designated by the department of human services or the county court for the county in which the facility is located.

Declaration made this _____ day of _____ (month, year).

I, _____, being at least eighteen years of age and of sound mind, willfully and voluntarily make known my desire that my life must not be artificially prolonged under the circumstances set forth below, and do hereby declare:

1. If at any time I should have an incurable condition caused by injury, disease, or illness certified to be a terminal condition by two physicians, and where the application of life-prolonging treatment would serve only to artificially prolong the process of my dying and my attending physician determines that my death is imminent whether or not life-prolonging treatment is utilized, I direct that such treatment be withheld or withdrawn, and that I be permitted to die naturally.

2. In the absence of my ability to give directions regarding the use of such life-prolonging treatment, it is my intention that this declaration be honored by my family and physicians as the final expression of my legal right to refuse medical or surgical treatment and accept the consequences of that refusal, which is death.

3. If I have been diagnosed as pregnant and that diagnosis is known to my physician, this declaration is not effective during the course of my pregnancy.

4. I understand the full import of this declaration and I am emotionally and mentally competent to make this declaration.

5. I understand that I may revoke this declaration at any time.

Signed _____

City, County, and State of Residence _____

The declarant has been personally known to me and I believe the declarant to be of sound mind. I am not related to the declarant by blood or marriage, nor would I be entitled to any portion of the declarant's estate upon the declarant's death. I am not the declarant's attending physician, a person who has a claim against any portion of the declarant's estate upon the declarant's death, or a person directly financially responsible for the declarant's medical care.

Witness _____

Witness _____

OKLAHOMA
1991; Public Health and Safety §3103

A living will in the State of Oklahoma must be substantially in the form provided, but may include additional directives consistent with the suggested form. The declarant must sign the living will document him or herself. The living will statute neither provides for nor precludes the designating of a health care proxy.

A living will in the State of Oklahoma must be witnessed by two adults and notarized by a notary public. The witnesses of the living will should not be

1) less than 21 years of age,
2) related to the declarant by blood or marriage,
3) a person who would inherit from the declarant under a will or codicil thereto or under the intestate laws of the state,
4) financially responsible for the medical care of the declarant,
5) a person who has a claim against the declarant or would have a claim against the declarant's estate,
6) the declarant's attending physician,
7) an employee of the declarant's physician or the health care facility in which the declarant is being treated at the time of the signing of the living will document, or
8) a patient in a health care facility in which the declarant is a patient.

DIRECTIVE TO PHYSICIANS

Directive made this _____ day of _____ (month, year).

I, _____, being of sound mind and twenty-one (21) years of age or older, willfully and voluntarily make known my desire that my life shall not be artificially prolonged under the circumstances set forth below, and do hereby declare:

1. If at any time I should have an incurable and irreversible condition caused by injury, disease, or illness certified to be a terminal condition by two physicians, I direct that life-sustaining procedures be withheld or withdrawn and that I be permitted to die naturally, if the application of life-sustaining procedures would only serve to artificially prolong the process of my dying and my attending physician determines that my death will occur within hours or days, whether or not life-sustaining procedures are utilized;

2. I understand that I am authorizing the withdrawal of any medical procedure or intervention that will only prolong the process of dying, when I have been found diagnosed as having a terminal condition (if declarant does not wish to authorize the withdrawal of any specific medical procedure or intervention specific directions shall be specified in the directive);

_____

3. I understand that when I have been diagnosed as having a terminal condition, the subject of the artificial administration of food and water that will only prolong the process of dying is of particular importance. Therefore, unless I sign this paragraph, I am not authorizing the withholding of nutrition or hydration (food or water):

a. I wish not to have artificial administration of food by tube or intravenous feeding,

(Signed) _____

b. I wish not to have artificial administration of water by tube or intravenously,

(Signed) _____

4. I understand that if I have given no specific directive concerning the artificial administration of food and water, it shall be presumed that I wish to receive nutrition and hydration to a degree sufficient to sustain life;

5. In the absence of my ability to give directions regarding the use of life-sustaining procedures, it is my intention

that this directive shall be honored by my family and physicians as the final expression of my legal right to refuse medical or surgical treatment, including, but not limited to, the administration of any life-sustaining procedures and accept the consequences of such refusal;

6. If I have been diagnosed as pregnant and that diagnosis is known to my physician, this directive shall have no force or effect during the course of my pregnancy;

7. I have been diagnosed and notified as having a terminal condition by _____, M.D. or D.O., whose address is _____, and whose telephone number is _____. I understand that if I have not filled in the name and address of the physician, it shall be presumed that I did not have a terminal condition when I made out this directive;

8. This directive shall be in effect until it is revoked;

9. I understand the full import of this directive and I am emotionally and mentally competent to make this directive; and

10. I understand that I may revoke this directive at any time.

Signed _____

City, County, and State of Residence _____

The declarant is personally known to me and I believe said declarant to be of sound mind. I am twenty-one (21) years of age or older, I am not related to the declarant by blood or marriage, nor would I be entitled to any portion of the estate of the declarant upon the death of said declarant, nor am I the attending physician of the declarant or an employee of the attending physician or a health care facility in which the declarant is a patient, or a patient in the health care facility in which the declarant is a patient, nor am I financially responsible for the medical care of the declarant, or any person who has a claim against any portion of the estate of the declarant upon the death of the declarant.

Witness _____

Witness _____

State of Oklahoma

County of _____

Before me, the undersigned authority, on this day personally appeared _____ (declarant), _____ (witness), and _____ (witness) whose names are subscribed to the foregoing instrument in their respective capacities, and, all of said persons being by me duly sworn, the declarant declared to me and to the said witnesses in my presence that said instrument is his or her "Directive to Physicians," and that the declarant has willingly and voluntarily made and executed it as the free act and deed of the declarant for the purposes therein expressed.

The foregoing instrument was acknowledged before me this _____ day of _____, 19_____.

Signed _____

Notary Public in and for _____ County, Oklahoma

My commission expires _____ day of _____, 19_____.

OREGON
1990; Guardians, Conservators, Power of Attorney; Trusts §127.610

A living will in the State of Oregon must be precisely in the form provided. The declarant must sign the living will document him or herself. The living will statute neither provides for nor precludes the designating of a health care proxy, but provisions for the designation of a power of attorney for health care appear elsewhere in the Oregon statutes.

A living will in the State of Oregon must be witnessed by two adults. The witnesses of the living will should not be

1) minors,

2) related to the declarant by blood or marriage,

3) a person who would inherit from the declarant under a will or codicil thereto or under the intestate laws of the state,

4) a person who has a claim against the declarant or would have a claim against the declarant's estate,

5) the declarant's attending physician, or

6) an employee of the declarant's physician or the health care facility in which the declarant is being treated at the time of the signing of the living will document.

In the State of Oregon, if the declarant is a patient in a long term care facility, one (1) of the witnesses to the living will must be an individual designated by the Department of Human Resources for the purpose of determining that the declarant is not so insulated from the voluntary decision-making role that the declarant is not capable of willfully and voluntarily executing a directive.

DIRECTIVE TO PHYSICIANS

Directive made this _____ day of _____ (month, year). I,

_____, being of sound mind, willfully and voluntarily make known my desire that my life shall not be artificially prolonged under the circumstances set forth below and do hereby declare:

1. If at any time I should have an incurable injury, disease, or illness certified to be a terminal condition by two physicians, one of whom is the attending physician, and where the application of life-sustaining procedures would serve only to artificially prolong the moment of my death and where my physician determines that my death is imminent whether or not life-sustaining procedures are utilized, I direct that such procedures be withheld or withdrawn, and that I be permitted to die naturally.

2. In the absence of my ability to give directions regarding the use of such life-sustaining procedures, it is my intention that this directive shall be honored by my family and physician(s) as the final expression of my legal right to refuse medical or surgical treatment and accept the consequences from such refusal.

3. I understand the full import of this directive and I am emotionally and mentally competent to make this declaration.

Signed _____

City, County, and State of Residence _____

I hereby witness this directive and attest that:

(1) I personally know the Declarant and believe the Declarant to be of sound mind.

(2) To the best of my knowledge, at the time of the execution of this directive, I:

    (a) Am not related to the Declarant by blood or marriage,

    (b) Do not have any claim on the estate of the Declarant,

    (c) Am not entitled to any portion of the Declarant's estate by any will or by operation of law, and

    (d) Am not a physician attending the Declarant, a person employed by a physician attending the Declarant, or a person employed by a health facility in which the Declarant is a patient.

(3) I understand that if I have not witnessed this directive in good faith I may be responsible for any damages that arise out of giving this directive its intended effect.

Witness _____

Witness _____

SOUTH CAROLINA

1990; Health §44-77-50

A living will in the State of South Carolina must be substantially in the form provided. The declarant must sign the living will document him or herself. The living will statute neither provides for nor precludes the designating of a health care proxy.

A living will in the State of South Carolina must be witnessed by two adults in the presence of an officer authorized to administer oaths under the laws of the state where the signing occurs. The witnesses of the living will should not be

1) minors,

2) related to the declarant by blood or marriage,

3) a person who would inherit from the declarant under a will or codicil thereto or under the intestate laws of the state,

4) financially responsible for the medical care of the declarant,

5) the beneficiary of a life insurance policy on the life of the declarant,

6) a person who has a claim against the declarant or would have a claim against the declarant's estate,

7) the declarant's attending physician,

8) an employee of the declarant's attending physician, or

9) both employees of the health facility in which the declarant is being treated at the time of the signing of the living will document.

In the State of South Carolina, if the declarant is a patient in a hospital or a skilled or intermediary care nursing facility, the signing of the living will should be witnessed by the State Ombudsman, Office of the Governor, with the ombudsman acting as one of the two witnesses and having the same qualifications as a witness as provided in this section.

STATE OF SOUTH CAROLINA
DECLARATION OF A DESIRE FOR A NATURAL DEATH

County of _____

I, _____, being at least eighteen years of age and a resident of and domiciled in the City of _____, County of _____, State of South Carolina, make this Declaration this _____ day of _____, 19_____.

I willfully and voluntarily make known my desire that no life-sustaining procedures be used to prolong my dying if my condition is terminal, and I declare:

If at any time I have a condition certified to be a terminal condition by two physicians who have personally examined me, one of whom is my attending physician, and the physicians have determined that my death will occur within a relatively short period of time without the use of life-sustaining procedures and where the application of life-sustaining procedures would serve only to prolong the dying process, I direct that the procedures be withheld or withdrawn, and that I be permitted to die naturally with only the administration of medication or the performance of any medical procedure necessary to provide me with comfort care.

In the absence of my ability to give directions regarding the use of such life-sustaining procedures, it is my intention that this Declaration be honored by my family and physicians and any health facility in which I may be a patient as the final expression of my legal right to refuse medical or surgical treatment, and I accept the consequences from the refusal.

I am aware that this Declaration authorizes a physician to withhold or withdraw life-sustaining procedures. I am emotionally and mentally competent to make this Declaration.

THIS DECLARATION MAY BE REVOKED:

(1) BY BEING DEFACED, TORN, OBLITERATED, OR OTHERWISE DESTROYED, IN EXPRESSION OF THE DECLARANT'S INTENT TO REVOKE, BY THE DECLARANT OR BY SOME PERSON IN THE PRESENCE OF AND BY THE DIRECTION OF THE DECLARANT. REVOCATION BY DESTRUCTION OF ONE OR MORE OF MULTIPLE ORIGINAL DECLARATIONS REVOKES ALL OF THE ORIGINAL DECLARATIONS. THE REVOCATION OF THE ORIGINAL DECLARATIONS ACTUALLY NOT DESTROYED BECOMES EFFECTIVE ONLY UPON COMMUNICATION TO THE ATTENDING PHYSICIAN. THE ATTENDING PHYSICIAN SHALL RECORD IN THE DECLARANT'S MEDICAL RECORD THE TIME AND DATE WHEN THE PHYSICIAN RECEIVED NOTIFICATION OF THE REVOCATION;

(2) BY A WRITTEN REVOCATION SIGNED AND DATED BY THE DECLARANT EXPRESSING HIS INTENT TO REVOKE. THE REVOCATION BECOMES EFFECTIVE ONLY UPON COMMUNICATION TO THE ATTENDING PHYSICIAN. THE ATTENDING PHYSICIAN SHALL RECORD IN THE DECLARANT'S MEDICAL RECORD THE TIME AND DATE WHEN THE PHYSICIAN RECEIVED NOTIFICATION OF THE WRITTEN REVOCATION;

(3) BY AN ORAL EXPRESSION BY THE DECLARANT OF HIS INTENT TO REVOKE THE DECLARATION. THE

REVOCATION BECOMES EFFECTIVE ONLY UPON COMMUNICATION TO THE ATTENDING PHYSICIAN BY THE DECLARANT. HOWEVER, AN ORAL REVOCATION MADE BY THE DECLARANT BECOMES EFFECTIVE UPON COMMUNICATION TO THE ATTENDING PHYSICIAN BY A PERSON OTHER THAN THE DECLARANT IF:

(a) THE PERSON WAS PRESENT WHEN THE ORAL REVOCATION WAS MADE;

(b) THE REVOCATION WAS COMMUNICATED TO THE PHYSICIAN WITHIN A REASONABLE TIME;

(c) THE PHYSICAL OR MENTAL CONDITION OF THE DECLARANT MAKES IT IMPOSSIBLE FOR THE PHYSICIAN TO CONFIRM THROUGH SUBSEQUENT CONVERSATION WITH THE DECLARANT THAT THE REVOCATION HAS OCCURRED.

THE ATTENDING PHYSICIAN SHALL RECORD IN THE PATIENT'S MEDICAL RECORD THE TIME, DATE, AND PLACE OF THE REVOCATION AND THE TIME, DATE, AND PLACE, IF DIFFERENT, OF WHEN HE RECEIVED NOTIFICATION OF THE REVOCATION. TO BE EFFECTIVE AS A REVOCATION, THE ORAL EXPRESSION CLEARLY MUST INDICATE A DESIRE THAT THE DECLARATION NOT BE GIVEN EFFECT OR THAT LIFE-SUSTAINING PROCEDURES BE ADMINISTERED;

(4) BY A WRITTEN, SIGNED, AND DATED REVOCATION OR AN ORAL REVOCATION BY A PERSON DESIGNATED BY THE DECLARANT IN THE DECLARATION, EXPRESSING THE DESIGNEE'S INTENT PERMANENTLY OR TEMPORARILY TO REVOKE THE DECLARATION. THE REVOCATION BECOMES EFFECTIVE ONLY UPON COMMUNICATION TO THE ATTENDING PHYSICIAN BY THE DESIGNEE. THE ATTENDING PHYSICIAN SHALL RECORD IN THE DECLARANT'S MEDICAL RECORD THE TIME, DATE, AND PLACE OF THE REVOCATION AND THE TIME, DATE, AND PLACE, IF DIFFERENT, OF WHEN HE RECEIVED NOTIFICATION OF THE REVOCATION. A DESIGNEE MAY REVOKE ONLY IF THE DECLARANT IS INCOMPETENT TO DO SO. IF THE DECLARANT WISHES TO DESIGNATE A PERSON WITH AUTHORITY TO REVOKE THE DECLARATION ON HIS BEHALF, THE NAME AND ADDRESS OF THAT PERSON MUST BE ENTERED BELOW:

Name of Designee _____

Address _____

Declarant _____

State of _____ AFFIDAVIT _____

County of _____ AFFIDAVIT _____

We, _____ and

_____, the undersigned witnesses to the foregoing Declaration, dated the

_____ day of _____, 19_____, being first duly sworn, declare to the undersigned authority, on the basis of our best information and belief, that the Declaration was on that date signed by the declarant as and for his Declaration of a Desire for a Natural Death in our presence and we, at his request and in his presence, and in the presence of each other, subscribe our names as witnesses on that date. The declarant is personally known to us, and we believe him to be of sound mind. Each of us affirms that he is qualified as a witness to this Declaration under the provisions of the South Carolina Death with Dignity Act in that he is not related to the declarant by blood or marriage, either as a spouse, lineal ancestor, descendant of the parents of the declarant, or spouse of any of them; nor directly financially responsible for the declarant's medical care; nor entitled to any portion of the declarant's estate upon his decease, whether under any will or as an heir by intestate succession; nor the beneficiary of a life insurance policy of the declarant; nor the declarant's attending physician; nor an employee of the attending physician; nor a person who has a claim against the declarant's decedent's estate as of this time. No more than one of us is an employee of a health facility in which the declarant is a patient. If the declarant is a patient in a hospital or skilled or intermediate care nursing facility at the date of execution of this Declaration at least one of us is an ombudsman designated by the State Ombudsman, Office of the Governor.

Witness _____

Witness _____

Subscribed before me by _____,

the declarant, and subscribed and sworn to before me by _____

and _____,

the witnesses, this _____ day of _____

19_____.

Notary Public for _____

My commission expires: _____

SEAL

SOUTH DAKOTA

1991; New in 1991 legislation. Not in statutes.

A living will in the State of South Dakota may, but need not, employ the form provided. The declarant is specifically allowed to direct another person to sign the declaration on his or her behalf if unable to do so themselves. The living will statute specifically refers to a power of attorney for health care decisions, but does not provide a form to do so. Provisions for designation of a power of attorney which covers health care decisions appear elsewhere in the South Dakota statutes.

A living will in the State of South Dakota must be witnessed by two adults. Witnessing before a notary is suggested but not required.

LIVING WILL DECLARATION

This is an important legal document. This document directs the medical treatment you are to receive in the event you are unable to participate in your own medical decisions and you are in a terminal condition. This document may state what kind of treatment you want or do not want to receive.

This document can control whether you live or die. Prepare this document carefully. If you use this form, read it completely. You may want to seek professional help to make sure the form does what you intend and is completed without mistakes.

This document will remain valid and in effect until and unless you revoke it. Review this document periodically to make sure it continues to reflect your wishes. You may amend or revoke this document at any time by notifying your physician and other health-care providers. You should give copies of this document to your physician and your family. This form is entirely optional. If you choose to use this form, please note that the form provides signature lines for you, the two witnesses whom you have selected, and a notary public.

TO MY FAMILY, PHYSICIANS, AND ALL THOSE CONCERNED WITH MY CARE:

I, _____, willfully and voluntarily make this declaration as a directive to be followed if I am in a terminal condition and become unable to participate in decisions regarding my medical care.

With respect to any life-sustaining treatment, I direct the following:

(Initial only one of the following optional directives if you agree. If you do not agree with any of the following directives, space is provided below for you to write your own directives.)

_____ NO LIFE-SUSTAINING TREATMENT. I direct that no life-sustaining treatment be provided. If life-sustaining treatment is begun, terminate it.

_____ TREATMENT FOR RESTORATION. Provide life-sustaining treatment only if and for so long as you believe treatment offers a reasonable possibility of restoring to me the ability to think and act for myself.

_____ TREAT UNLESS PERMANENTLY UNCONSCIOUS. If you believe that I am permanently unconscious and are satisfied that this condition is irreversible, then do not provide me with life-sustaining treatment, and if life-sustaining treatment is being provided to me, terminate it. If and so long as you believe that treatment has a reasonable possibility of restoring consciousness to me, then provide life-sustaining treatment.

141

_____ MAXIMUM TREATMENT. Preserve my life as long as possible, but do not provide treatment that is not in accordance with accepted medical standards as then in effect.

(Artificial nutrition and hydration is food and water provided by means of a nasogastric tube or tubes inserted into the stomach, intestines, or veins. If you do not wish to receive this form of treatment, you must initial the statement below which reads: "I intend to include this treatment among the 'life-sustaining treatment' that may be withheld or withdrawn.")

With respect to artificial nutrition and hydration, I wish to make clear that

(Initial only one)

_____ I intend to include this treatment among the "life-sustaining treatment" that may be withheld or withdrawn.

_____ I do not intend to include this treatment among the "life-sustaining treatment" that may be withheld or withdrawn.

(If you do not agree with any of the printed directives and want to write your own, or if you want to write directives in addition to the printed provisions, or if you want to express some of your other thoughts, you can do so here.)

_____

_____

_____

_____

_____

_____

Date: _____

(Your Signature) _____

(Your Address) _____

(Type or Print Your Signature) _____

The declarant voluntarily signed this document in my presence.

Witness _____

Address _____

Witness _____

Address _____

On this the _____ day of _____, _____, the declarant,

_____, and witnesses,

_____, and _____,

personally appeared before the undersigned officer and signed the foregoing instrument in my presence. Dated this _____ day of _____, _____.

Notary Public _____

My commission expires: _____

TENNESSEE
1990; Wills §32-11-105

A living will in the State of Tennessee may, but need not, employ the form provided. The declarant must sign the living will document him or herself. The living will statute neither provides for nor precludes the designating of a health care proxy, but provisions for the designation of a power of attorney for health care appear elsewhere in the Tennessee statutes. It also allows the addition to the declaration which reads: "I authorize the withholding of artificially provided food, water, or other nourishment or fluids."

A living will in the State of Tennessee must be witnessed by two adults. The witnesses of the living will should not be

1) minors,

2) related to the declarant by blood or marriage,

3) a person who would inherit from the declarant under a will or codicil thereto or under the intestate laws of the state,

4) a person who has a claim against the declarant or would have a claim against the declarant's estate,

5) the declarant's attending physician, or

6) an employee of the declarant's physician or the health care facility in which the declarant is being treated at the time of the signing of the living will document.

LIVING WILL

I, _____, willfully and voluntarily make known my desire that my dying shall not be artificially prolonged under the circumstances set forth below, and do hereby declare:

If at any time I should have a terminal condition and my attending physician has determined that there is no reasonable expectation of recovery and which, as a medical probability, will result in my death, regardless of the use or discontinuance of medical treatment implemented for the purpose of sustaining life, or the life process, I direct that medical care be withheld or withdrawn, and that I be permitted to die naturally with only the administration of medications or the performance of any medical procedure deemed necessary to provide me with comfortable care or to alleviate pain.

ARTIFICIALLY PROVIDED NOURISHMENT AND FLUIDS: By checking the appropriate line below I specifically:

_____ authorize the withholding or withdrawal of artificially provided food, water, or other nourishment or fluids.

_____ *DO NOT* authorize the withholding or withdrawal of artificially provided food, water, or other nourishment or fluids.

ORGAN DONOR CERTIFICATION: Notwithstanding my previous declaration relative to the withholding or withdrawal of life-prolonging procedures, if as indicated below I have expressed my desire to donate my organs and/or tissues for transplantation, or any of them as specifically designated herein, I do direct my attending physician, if I have been determined dead according to Tennessee Code Annotated, Section 68-3-501(b), to maintain me on artificial support systems only for the period of time required to maintain the viability of and to remove such organs and/or tissues. By checking the appropriate line below I specifically:

_____ desire to donate my organs and/or tissues for transplantation.

_____ desire to donate my _____.

(Insert specific organs and/or tissues for transplantation.)

_____ *DO NOT* desire to donate my organs and/or tissues for transplantation.

In the absence of my ability to give directions regarding my medical care, it is my intention that this declaration shall be honored by my family and physician as the final expression of my legal right to refuse medical or surgical treatment and accept the consequences from such refusal.

The definitions of terms used herein shall be as set forth in the Tennessee Right to Natural Death Act, Tennessee Code Annotated, Section 32-11-103. I understand the full import of this declaration, and I am emotionally and mentally competent to make this declaration. In acknowledgment whereof, I do hereinafter affix my signature on this the _____ day of _____, 19_____.

Declarant _____

We, the subscribing witnesses hereto, are personally acquainted with and subscribe our names hereto at the request of the declarant, an adult, whom we believe to be of sound mind, fully aware of the action taken herein and its possible consequence.

We, the undersigned witnesses, further declare that we are not related to the declarant by blood or marriage; that we are not entitled to any portion of the estate of the declarant upon his decease under any will or codicil thereto presently existing or by operation of law then existing; that we are not the attending physician, an employee of the attending physician or a health facility in which the declarant is a patient; and that we are not a person who, at the present time, has a claim against any portion of the estate of the declarant upon his death.

Witness _____

Witness _____

Subscribed, sworn to, and acknowledged before me by _____,

the declarant, and subscribed and sworn to before me by _____ and

_____, witnesses, this _____ day of _____,

19_____.

_____

Notary Public

144

TEXAS

1991; Health and Safety Code §672.003

A living will in the State of Texas may, but need not, employ the form provided. The declarant must sign the living will document him or herself. The living will statute specifically allows the delegation of a health care proxy, but does not provide a form to do so. A form for a power of attorney for health care is available in other provisions of the Texas statutes.

A living will in the State of Texas must be witnessed by two adults. The witnesses of the living will should not be

1) minors,

2) related to the declarant by blood or marriage,

3) a person who would inherit from the declarant under a will or codicil thereto or under the intestate laws of the state,

4) a person who has a claim against the declarant or would have a claim against the declarant's estate,

5) the declarant's attending physician,

6) a patient of a health care facility in which the declarant is a patient or resident, or

7) an employee of the declarant's physician or the health care facility in which the declarant is being treated at the time of the signing of the living will document.

DIRECTIVE TO PHYSICIANS

Directive made this _____ day of _____ (month, year).

I, _____, being of sound mind, willfully and voluntarily make known my desire that my life shall not be artificially prolonged under the circumstances set forth below, and do hereby declare:

1. If at any time I should have an incurable or irreversible condition caused by injury, disease, or illness certified to be a terminal condition by two physicians, and where the application of life-sustaining procedures would serve only to artificially prolong the moment of my death and where my attending physician determines that my death is imminent or will result within a relatively short time without application of life-sustaining procedures, I direct that such procedures be withheld or withdrawn, and that I be permitted to die naturally.

2. In the absence of my ability to give directions regarding the use of such life-sustaining procedures, it is my intention that this directive shall be honored by my family and physicians as the final expression of my legal right to refuse medical or surgical treatment and accept the consequences from such refusal.

3. If I have been diagnosed as pregnant and that diagnosis is known to my physician, this directive shall have no force or effect during the course of my pregnancy.

4. This directive shall be in effect until it is revoked.

5. I understand the full import of this directive and I am emotionally and mentally competent to make this directive.

6. I understand that I may revoke this directive at any time.

Signed _____

City, County, and State of Residence _____

I am not related to the declarant by blood or marriage; nor would I be entitled to any portion of the declarant's estate on his decease; nor am I the attending physician of the declarant or an employee of the attending physician; nor am I a patient in the health care facility in which the declarant is a patient, or any person who has a claim against any portion of the estate of the declarant upon his decease. Furthermore, if I am an employee of a health facility in which the declarant is a patient, I am not involved in providing direct patient care to the declarant nor am I directly involved in the financial affairs of the health facility.

Witness _____

Witness _____

UTAH

1990; Uniform Probate Code §75-2-1104

A living will in the State of Utah must be substantially in the form provided. The declarant is specifically allowed to direct another person to sign the declaration on his or her behalf if unable to do so themselves. The living will statute provides a form provision for the delegation of a health care proxy.

A living will in the State of Utah must be witnessed by two adults. The witnesses of the living will should not be

1) less than 18 years of age,

2) the person who signed the declaration for the declarant,

3) related to the declarant by blood or marriage,

4) a person who would inherit from the declarant under a will or codicil thereto or under the intestate laws of the state,

5) financially responsible for the medical care of the declarant, or

6) any agent of any health care facility in which the declarant is a patient at the time the directive is executed.

DIRECTIVE TO PHYSICIANS AND PROVIDERS OF MEDICAL SERVICES

(Pursuant to Section 75-2-1104 UCA)

This directive is made this _____ day of _____, _____.

1. I, _____, being of sound mind, willfully and voluntarily make known my desire that my life not be artificially prolonged by life-sustaining procedures except as I may otherwise provide in this directive.

2. I declare that if at any time I should have an injury, disease, or illness, which is certified in writing to be a terminal condition by two physicians who have personally examined me, and in the opinion of those physicians the application of life-sustaining procedures would serve only to unnaturally prolong the moment of my death and to unnaturally postpone or prolong the dying process, I direct that these procedures be withheld or withdrawn and my death be permitted to occur naturally.

3. I expressly intend this directive to be a final expression of my legal right to refuse medical or surgical treatment and to accept the consequences from this refusal which shall remain in effect notwithstanding my future inability to give current medical directions to treating physicians and other providers of medical services.

4. I understand that the term "life-sustaining procedure" does not include the administration of medication or sustenance, or the performance of any medical procedure deemed necessary to provide comfort care, or to alleviate pain, except to the extent I specify below that any of these procedures be considered life-sustaining.

5. I reserve the right to give current medical directions to physicians and other providers of medical services so long as I am able, even though these directions may conflict with the above written directive that life-sustaining procedures be withheld or withdrawn.

6. I understand the full import of this directive and declare that I am emotionally and mentally competent to make this directive.

Declarant's signature _____

City, County, and State of Residence _____

We witnesses certify that each of us is 18 years of age or older and each personally witnessed the declarant sign or direct the signing of this directive; that we are acquainted with the declarant and believe him to be of sound mind; that the declarant's desires are as expressed above; that neither of us is a person who signed the above directive on behalf of the declarant; that we are not related to the declarant by blood or marriage nor are we entitled to any portion of declarant's estate according to the laws of intestate succession of this state or under any will or codicil of declarant; that we are not directly financially responsible for declarant's medical care; and that we are not agents of any health care facility in which the declarant may be a patient at the time of signing this directive.

Signature of Witness _____

Address of Witness _____

Signature of Witness _____

Address of Witness _____

VERMONT
1990; Health §5253

A living will in the State of Vermont may, but need not, be in the form provided. The declarant must sign the living will document him or herself. The living will statute neither provides for nor precludes the designating of a health care proxy, but provisions for the designation of a power of attorney for health care appear elsewhere in the Vermont statutes.

A living will in the State of Vermont must be witnessed by two adults. The witnesses of the living will should not be

1) minors,
2) spouse,
3) a person who would inherit from the declarant under a will or codicil thereto or under the intestate laws of the state,
4) a person who has a claim against the declarant or would have a claim against the declarant's estate,
5) the declarant's attending physician, or
6) a person under the control of the declarant's attending physician.

TERMINAL CARE DOCUMENT

To my family, my physician, my lawyer, my clergyman. To any medical facility in whose care I happen to be. To any individual who may become responsible for my health, welfare, or affairs.

Death is as much a reality as birth, growth, maturity, and old age—it is the one certainty of life. If the time comes when I, _____, can no longer take part in decisions of my own future, let this statement stand as an expression of my wishes, while I am still of sound mind.

If the situation should arise in which I am in a terminal state and there is no reasonable expectation of my recovery, I direct that I be allowed to die a natural death and that my life not be prolonged by extraordinary measures. I do, however, ask that medication be mercifully administered to me to alleviate suffering even though this may shorten my remaining life.

This statement is made after careful consideration and is in accordance with my strong convictions and beliefs. I want the wishes and directions here expressed carried out to the extent permitted by law. Insofar as they are not legally enforceable, I hope that those to whom this will is addressed will regard themselves as morally bound by these provisions.

Signed: _____

Date: _____

Witness: _____

Witness: _____

Copies of this request have been given to:

_____

_____

_____

VIRGINIA
1990; Professions and Occupations §54.1-2984

A living will in the State of Virginia may, but need not, employ the forms provided. The declarant may only make an oral declaration after being told he or she has a terminal disease. The living will statute specifically allows the delegation of a health care proxy, but does not provide a form to do so.

A living will in the State of Virginia must be witnessed by two adults.

Declaration made this _____ day of _____ (month, year). I, _____, willfully and voluntarily make known my desire and do hereby declare:

CHOOSE ONLY ONE OF THE NEXT TWO PARAGRAPHS AND CROSS THROUGH THE OTHER

If at any time I should have a terminal condition, and I am comatose, incompetent, or otherwise mentally or physically incapable of communication, I designate _____ to make a decision on my behalf as to whether life-prolonging procedures shall be withheld or withdrawn. In the event that my designee decides that such procedures should be withheld or withdrawn, I wish to be permitted to die naturally with only the administration of medication or the performance of any medical procedure deemed necessary to provide me with comfort care or to alleviate pain. (OPTION: I specifically direct that the following procedures or treatments be provided to me: _____.)

OR

If at any time I should have a terminal condition where the application of life-prolonging procedures would serve only to artificially prolong the dying process, I direct that such procedures be withheld or withdrawn, and that I be permitted to die naturally with only the administration of medication or the performance of any medical procedure deemed necessary to provide me with comfort care or to alleviate pain. (OPTION: I specifically direct that the following procedures or treatments be provided to me: _____.)

In the absence of my ability to give directions regarding the use of such life-prolonging procedures, it is my intention that this declaration shall be honored by my family and physician as the final expression of my legal right to refuse medical or surgical treatment and accept the consequences of such refusal.

I understand the full import of this declaration and I am emotionally and mentally competent to make this declaration.

(Signed) _____

The declarant is known to me and I believe him or her to be of sound mind.

Witness _____

Witness _____

WASHINGTON
1991; Public Health and Safety §70.122.030

A living will in the State of Washington must be substantially in the form provided, but may include additional directives consistent with the suggested form. The declarant must sign the living will document him or herself. The living will statute neither provides for nor precludes the designating of a health care proxy. The durable power of attorney statute specifically allows health care decisions, but may or may not allow the withholding or withdrawal of life support systems.

A living will in the State of Washington must be witnessed by two adults. The witnesses of the living will should not be

1) minors,

2) related to the declarant by blood or marriage,

3) a person who would inherit from the declarant under a will or codicil thereto or under the intestate laws of the state,

4) a person who has a claim against the declarant or would have a claim against the declarant's estate,

5) the declarant's attending physician, or

6) an employee of the declarant's physician or the health care facility in which the declarant is being treated at the time of the signing of the living will document.

A copy of the completed form should be made part of the declarant's medical records.

DIRECTIVE TO PHYSICIANS

Directive made this _____ day of _____ (month, year).

I, _____, being of sound mind, willfully and voluntarily make known my desire that my life shall not be artificially prolonged under the circumstances set forth below, and do hereby declare that:

(a) If at any time I should have an incurable injury, disease, or illness certified to be a terminal condition by two physicians, and where the application of life-sustaining procedures would serve only to artificially prolong the moment of my death and where my physician determines that my death is imminent whether or not life-sustaining procedures are utilized, I direct that such procedures be withheld or withdrawn, and that I be permitted to die naturally.

(b) In the absence of my ability to give directions regarding the use of such life-sustaining procedures, it is my intention that this directive shall be honored by my family and physician(s) as the final expression of my legal right to refuse medical or surgical treatment and I accept the consequences from such refusal.

(c) If I have been diagnosed as pregnant and that diagnosis is known to my physician, this directive shall have no force or effect during the course of my pregnancy.

(d) I understand the full import of this directive and I am emotionally and mentally competent to make this directive.

Signed _____

City, County, and State of Residence _____

The declarer has been personally known to me and I believe him or her to be of sound mind.

Witness _____

Witness _____

WEST VIRGINIA
1991; Public Health §16-30-3

A living will in the State of West Virginia may, but need not, be in the form provided, and may include additional directives consistent with the living will statute. The declarant is specifically allowed to direct another person to sign the declaration on his or her behalf if unable to do so themselves. The living will statute neither provides for nor precludes the designating of a health care proxy, but provisions for the designation of a medical power of attorney appear elsewhere in the West Virginia statutes.

A living will in the State of West Virginia must be witnessed by two adults, who attest as indicated below before a notary public. The witnesses of the living will should not be

1) less than 18 years of age,

2) the person who signed the declaration for the declarant,

3) related to the declarant by blood or marriage,

4) a person who would inherit from the declarant under a will or codicil thereto or under the intestate laws of the state,

5) financially responsible for the medical care of the declarant,

6) a person who has a claim against the declarant or would have a claim against the declarant's estate,

7) the declarant's health care proxy or successor thereto, or

8) the declarant's attending physician.

LIVING WILL

Living will made this _____ day of _____ (month, year). I, _____, being of sound mind, willfully and voluntarily declare that in the absence of my ability to give directions regarding the use of life-prolonging intervention, it is my desire that my dying shall not be artificially prolonged under the following circumstances:

If at any time I should be certified by two physicians who have personally examined me, one of whom is my attending physician, to have a terminal condition or to be in a persistent vegetative state, I direct that life-prolonging intervention that would serve solely to artificially prolong the dying process or maintain me in a persistent vegetative state be withheld or withdrawn, and that I be permitted to die naturally with only the administration of medication or the performance of any other medical procedure deemed necessary to keep me comfortable and alleviate pain.

SPECIAL DIRECTIVES OR LIMITATIONS ON THIS DECLARATION (if none, write "none."):

_____

It is my intention that this living will be honored as the final expression of my legal right to refuse medical or surgical treatment and accept the consequences resulting from such refusal.

I understand the full import of this living will.

Signed _____

Address _____

_____

I did not sign the declarant's signature above for or at the direction of the declarant. I am at least eighteen years of age and am not related to the declarant by blood or marriage, entitled to any portion of the estate of the declarant according to the laws of intestate succession of the state of the declarant's domicile or to the best of my knowledge under any will of declarant or codicil thereto, or directly financially responsible for declarant's medical care. I am not the declarant's attending physician, or the declarant's health care representative, proxy, or successor health care representative under a medical power of attorney.

Witness _____

Address _____

_____

Witness _____

Address _____

State of _____

County of _____

The foregoing instrument was acknowledged before me this _____ (date) by the declarant and by the two witnesses whose signatures appear above.

My commission expires: _____

Signature of Notary Public _____

WISCONSIN

1990; Public Health §154.03

A living will in the State of Wisconsin must be precisely in the form provided. The declarant is specifically allowed to direct another person to sign the declaration on his or her behalf if unable to do so themselves. The living will statute neither provides for nor precludes the designating of a health care proxy, but provisions for the designation of a power of attorney for health care appear elsewhere in the Wisconsin statutes.

A living will in the State of Wisconsin must be witnessed by two adults. The witnesses of the living will should not be

1) minors,

2) related to the declarant by blood or marriage,

3) a person who would inherit from the declarant under a will or codicil thereto or under the intestate laws of the state,

4) the declarant's attending physician, attending nurse, or the attending medical staff,

5) a person who has a claim against the declarant or would have a claim against the declarant's estate, or

6) an employee of the declarant's physician or the inpatient health care facility in which the declarant is being treated at the time of the signing of the living will document.

DECLARATION TO PHYSICIANS

Declaration made this _____ day of _____ (month), _____ (year).

1. I, _____, being of sound mind, willfully and voluntarily state my desire that my dying may not be artificially prolonged if I have an incurable injury or illness certified to be a terminal condition by two physicians who have personally examined me, one of whom is my attending physician, and if the physicians have determined that my death is imminent, so that the application of life-sustaining procedures would serve only to prolong artificially the dying process. Under these circumstances, I direct that life-sustaining procedures be withheld or withdrawn and that I be permitted to die naturally, with only:

    a. The continuation of nutritional support and fluid maintenance; and

    b. The alleviation of pain by administering medication or other medical procedure.

2. If I am unable to give directions regarding the use of life-sustaining procedures, I intend that my family and physician honor this declaration as the final expression of my legal right to refuse medical or surgical treatment and to accept the consequences from this refusal.

3. If I have been diagnosed as pregnant and my physician knows of this diagnosis, this declaration has no effect during the course of my pregnancy.

4. This declaration takes effect immediately.

I understand this declaration and I am emotionally and mentally competent to make this declaration.

Signed _____

Address _____

I know the declarant personally and I believe him or her to be of sound mind. I am not related to the declarant by blood or marriage, and am not entitled to any portion of the declarant's estate under any will of the declarant. I am neither the declarant's attending physician, the attending nurse, the attending medical staff, nor an employee of the attending physician or of the inpatient health care facility in which the declarant may be a patient and I have no claim against the declarant's estate at this time, except that, if I am not a health care provider who is involved in the medical care of the declarant, I may be an employee of the inpatient health care facility regardless of whether or not the facility may have a claim against the estate of the declarant.

Witness _____

Witness _____

This declaration is executed as provided in chapter 154, Wisconsin Statutes.

WYOMING

1990; Public Health and Safety §35-22-101

A living will in the State of Wyoming may, but need not, employ the form provided. The declarant is specifically allowed to direct another person to sign the declaration on his or her behalf if unable to do so themselves. The living will statute provides a form provision for the delegation of Power of Attorney for Health Care.

A living will in the State of Wyoming must be witnessed by two adults. The witnesses of the living will should not be

1) minors,

2) the person who signed the declaration for the declarant,

3) related to the declarant by blood or marriage,

4) a person who would inherit from the declarant under a will or codicil thereto or under the intestate laws of the state, or

5) financially responsible for the medical care of the declarant.

DECLARATION

Declaration made this _____ day of _____ (month, year). I, _____, being of sound mind, willfully and voluntarily make known my desire that my dying shall not be artificially prolonged under the circumstances set forth below, do hereby declare: If at any time I should have an incurable injury, disease, or other illness certified to be a terminal condition by two (2) physicians who have personally examined me, one (1) of whom shall be my attending physician, and the physicians have determined that my death will occur whether or not life-sustaining procedures are utilized and where the application of life-sustaining procedures would serve only to artificially prolong the dying process, I direct that such procedures be withheld or withdrawn, and that I be permitted to die naturally with only the administration of medication or the performance of any medical procedure deemed necessary to provide me with comfort care. If, in spite of this declaration, I am comatose or otherwise unable to make treatment decisions for myself, I HEREBY designate _____ to make treatment decisions for me.

In the absence of my ability to give directions regarding the use of life-sustaining procedures, it is my intention that this declaration shall be honored by my family and physician(s) and agent as the final expression of my legal right to refuse medical or surgical treatment and accept the consequences from this refusal. I understand the full import of this declaration and I am emotionally and mentally competent to make this declaration.

Signed _____

City, County, and State of Residence _____

The declarant has been personally known to me and I believe him or her to be of sound mind. I did not sign the declarant's signature above for or at the direction of the declarant. I am not related to the declarant by blood or marriage, entitled to any portion of the estate of the declarant according to the laws of intestate succession or under any will of declarant or codicil thereto, or directly financially responsible for declarant's medical care.

Witness _____

Witness _____

DELAWARE: Has a Living Will statute.

MASSACHUSETTS: Does not have a Living Will statute at the time of the writing of this book, but there are provisions for the designation of a power of attorney for health care in the Massachusetts statutes.

MICHIGAN: Does not have a Living Will statute at the time of the writing of this book, but there are provisions for the designation of a power of attorney for health care in the Michigan statutes.

NEBRASKA: No Living Will statute as of the time of the writing of this book.

NEW JERSEY: Has a Living Will statute.

NEW MEXICO: 1989; Health and Safety §24-7-3

A Living Will in the State of New Mexico may employ any form favored by the declarant. The declarant must sign the Living Will document himself or herself. The living will statute neither provides for nor precludes the designating of a health-care proxy.

A Living Will in the State of New Mexico must be witnessed by two credible witnesses who attest in writing that they saw the declarant sign the will in his or her presence and the presence of each other.

NEW YORK: Does not have a Living Will statute at the time of the writing of this book, but there are provisions for the designation of a power of attorney for health care and for the writing of an order not to resuscitate in the New York statutes.

OHIO: No Living Will statute as of the time of the writing of this book. The Ohio statutes do provide for a durable power of attorney for health care with the authority to withhold or withdraw therapy from a principal who has a terminal condition.

PENNSYLVANIA: Does not have a Living Will statute at the time of the writing of this book. There are provisions for the designation of a power of attorney for health care in the Pennsylvania statutes, but may or may not allow the withholding or withdrawal of life-support systems.

RHODE ISLAND: While on press, Rhode Island passed a Living Will Statute. Please send self-addressed envelope to publisher for free form.

OTHER AREAS WITHOUT LIVING WILL FORMS

COMMONWEALTH OF PUERTO RICO
VIRGIN ISLANDS
GUAM

INDEX

A

abdominal aneurysm, 40
A.B. v C., 41
Action of The Council for Christian Social Action of the
    United Church of Christ, 48
activation of Living Will, 22, 27
age, and cessation of treatment, 54
AIDS, 15
Alabama, form declaration for, 75
Alaska:
    form declaration for, 77
    URTIA-based legislation in, 24
Alzheimer's disease, 15
American Jewish Congress, 48–49
American Medical Association (AMA), 53–54
amputation, refusal of, 14, 34
amyotrophic lateral sclerosis (Lou Gehrig's disease),
    cessation of treatment approved for, 40, 42
antibiotics, 14
appellate court, 18
Aqudath Israel of America, 49
Arizona:
    form declaration for, 79–80
    Rasmussen v Fleming, 34, 35, 36, 38, 39
Arkansas, 39
    form declaration for, 81
    URTIA-based legislation in, 24
assisted suicide, 31
atherosclerosis, 40
attending physician, URTIA definition of, 24
auto accidents, 39

B

Barber v Superior Court, 39
Barry, Guardianship of, 34, 35
Bartling v Superior Court, 35, 40
Batten's disease, cessation of treatment approved for, 39
best interest approach, 43
bioethics committees, 42

Blodgett, In re, 40
blood transfusions, 36
Bludworth, John F. Kennedy Hospital v, 36
Botsford, Union Pacific Railway Co. v, 33
Bouvia v County of Riverside, 34, 36, 40
Boyd, In re, 35
brain damage, 40, 41
Brophy, New England Mount Sinai Hospital v, 34, 35, 38,
    39, 42
Browning, In re Guardianship of, 41

C

California, 33
    Barber, 39
    Bartling, 35, 40
    Bouvia, 34, 36, 40
    Drabick, 34, 38
    form declaration for, 83–84
    Living Will statutes in, 38
    medical malpractice litigation in, 18
    priority and precedence in, 19
    reaffirmation of directives in, 52
California Natural Death Act, 13–14, 18, 24
cardio-pulmonary resuscitation (CPR), 51
Cardoza, Benjamin, 33–34
Catholics, 48
CAT scans, 14
Caulk, In re, 36
cerebral palsy, cessation of treatment approved for, 40
Cesarean section, 36
children:
    financial support for, 36
    in PVS, 53
    treatment denied to, 36
chronic, progressive, irreversible condition, 56
circuit court, 17, 18, 19
civil rights, 12
clear and convincing evidence, 20
    for acquisition of court approval, 42
    as required by states, 43

163